Reincarnation
in Christianity

Reincarnation in Christianity

*A New Vision of the Role of
Rebirth in Christian Thought*

GEDDES MacGREGOR

*Emeritus Distinguished Professor of Philosophy,
University of Southern California*

This publication made possible with the assistance
of the Kern Foundation

**The Theosophical Publishing House
Wheaton, Ill. U.S.A.
Madras, India/London, England**

Second Quest printing 1981, published by The Theosophical
Publishing House, a department of The Theosophical Society in
America. Inquiries for permission to reproduce all, or portions
of this book, should be addressed to Quest Books, 306 West
Geneva Road, Wheaton, Illinois 60187

Library of Congress Cataloging in Publication Data

MacGregor, Geddes.
   Reincarnation in Christianity.
   (A Quest book)
   Bibliography: p.200
   Includes index.
   1. Christianity and reincarnation. I. Title
BR115.R4M3   236'.2   77-20925
ISBN 0-8356-0504-3
ISBN 0-8356-0501-9 pbk.

Printed in the United States of America

To the Dean and Faculty of Religious Studies of McGill University who elected me to give the Birks Lectures out of which this book grew, and to all my students there and everywhere in gratitude for their critical zest and most of all for the knowledge of their abiding love.

CONTENTS

CONTENTS

PREFACE

Reincarnation is one of the most fascinating ideas in the history of religion, as it is also one of the most recurrent themes in the literature of the world. It is widely assumed to be foreign to the Christian heritage and especially alien to the Hebrew roots of biblical thought. That assumption is questionable.

This book is developed for the general reader out of the Birks Lectures I delivered at McGill University, entitled *The Christening of Karma*. It is an inquiry, certainly not a polemic for or against reincarnationism. Evidence does exist to suggest that the notion is incompatible with both Judaism and Christianity. Other evidence, however, may be adduced to support the view that a form of it might even be a doctrine within the apostolic tradition, the recovery of which could be essential to the plenitude of the Christian faith. In the one case, presumably the faithful should be warned against it. In the other case, the rehabilitation of the doctrine would seem to be a matter of urgency. More likely, and surely exciting enough, would be the conclusion, if warranted, that a form of reincarnationism (perhaps such as some of the early Fathers called *metensomatosis*) might be a viable option for those who, seeking to be faithful to Christian orthodoxy, look to the Bible as their primary warrant and to Church tradition as their guide to its interpretation. This book is an inquiry into the grounds, if any, on which such a conclusion might be legitimately reached. Though I do not obtrude my personal sympathies, neither do I disguise them.

Since some readers will be interested in the idea of reincarnationism for its own sake, a bibliography, partially annotated, is provided.

Geddes MacGregor

I

THE UNIVERSAL APPEAL OF REINCARNATION

I held that when a person dies
His soul returns again to earth;
Arrayed in some new flesh-disguise,
Another mother gives him birth.
With sturdier limbs and brighter brain
The old soul takes the roads again.

John Masefield, *A Creed*

Of all ideas in the history of religion, none is more universal in its appeal than is that of reincarnation. It appears both in very primitive forms of religion and in highly developed ones. True, it seems to prosper better in some religious climates than in others. Everyone knows that in India it is inseparable from the cultural outlook. It is part of the mental furniture of the whole sub-continent. Yet India is by no means its only home. Even in those civilizations in which, for one reason or another, it has been frowned on, it has emerged in unlikely corners and in unexpected ways, as the deep roots of an old tree send forth shoots far from the main trunk. Christianity and Judaism are no exceptions. We shall see how persistently it has cropped up in various crannies along the Christian Way, from the earliest times down to the present. No less unexpectedly has it flourished in Judaism. Poets have favored it:

the theme recurs in Goethe, in Wordsworth, in Browning, in Blake, in Yeats, in Masefield, and in many others. Wherever occidental thinkers have learned to love the Christian Way well enough to strip off dead dogma without destroying living vision, it has found a place in the Church's life.

The modern philosophical and scientific objections to the classic presentations of reincarnationism are indeed formidable.[1] We shall consider them in a special chapter. First let us ask: wherein lies the peculiar appeal of the notion that one's present life is but one of a series? It is a notion that is entertained even by many who do not take much interest in religious ideas and to whom other doctrines, whether of immortality or of resurrection, mean little or nothing. Why should it so captivate even those who seem to be conceptually least prepared for it?

I ask the reader to be particularly clear on one point. In presenting the following eight considerations as among the most telling, I am not suggesting that they should compel either denial or assent. At this stage we are less concerned with the truth of the notion than with its meaning. We should first see what the notion means, then whether it is as plausible as it is intelligible. We may then go on to assess any plausibility that we may find in it.

First, then, the notion is more satisfying to many people, both morally and intellectually, than is any proposal that appears to entail an arbitrary "divine judgment". Karma is automatic. There is no arbitrariness or subjectivity in it. That does not necessarily exclude (though historically it has often done so) the notion of mercy and forgiveness. God *might* be seen as finding ways of overcoming the moral law of karma, as he is seen by some to find ways of overcoming nature, not by destroying or injuring it but by going beyond our apprehension of it. Karma, which is intelligible to the human mind by analogy with scientific "laws", could be seen as providing the basis, as does the Torah, of the ways of God to man. The natural sciences, such as physics and chemistry, help us to understand the way things are. So the cosmic moral law of karma might be seen to help us to understand how things are in the moral order. The learned may call this way of looking at things "neo-Gnostic"; but while it certainly can be developed along Gnostic lines, and very often indeed has been so developed in the history of human thought, so as to preclude the exercise of God's will and the operation of his love, it need not be so developed. It can stand while allowing room for the surprising acts of God. So while it may not be indigenous to those religions that stress the will of God acting freely in history (e.g. Judaism, Christianity and Islam), it need not be wholly incompatible with them. An analogy might be drawn from our attitude to the sciences. What physicists and chemists and biologists say *may* be interpreted nihilistically; but it need not be. As it need not exclude the possibility of a theistic interpretation, neither need a karmic view of the moral realm exclude an orthodox Christian or Jewish or Muslim view of the sovereignty of God's will.

Second, reincarnation accords well with much that we now know about evolution in the world of biology and physics. The notion that the struggle for biological development has a counterpart in the struggle for moral development is at least plausible. As some of the early evolutionists saw their discovery as a "tooth and claw" principle, the "survival of the fittest", so the karmic principle may be interpreted as a struggle for the development of a might-is-right sort of moral power; but it need not be. It need no more be so interpreted than must religion, which ideologically begins as primitive fear (*primus in orbe deos fecit timor*), be precluded from eventually transcending that fear.

Third, the notion that we reap what we sow, be it now or a trillion lives later, is eminently congenial to those who attach importance to the notion of human freedom of choice. For while the karmic principle is as inexorable as are the "laws" of physics and genetics, we are by no means to be seen as helplessly imprisoned in its clutches. On the contrary, we create our own karma by our own acts. Karma is the given (it is *jeté là, comme ça*, as Sartre calls the state of affairs we encounter in human life), and our task is to extricate ourselves from it (as in the great "prison" *motif* of modern existentialism) by surmounting it and so creating new and hopefully better karma. I have created the prison from which I must now extricate myself.

Fourth, the universality of the notion in the history of religion is not a negligible element in its appeal to thoughtful and educated people. Again, that does not mean that it need be the last word in the history of religious ideas. Nevertheless, no serious and historically-minded student of religion will lightly write it off. At least it must have expressed something important in the religious consciousness of humankind. If it is to be accounted outmoded, what precisely takes its place? Whatever that is alleged to be, does it effectively encompass and supersede the allegedly outmoded notion of reincarnation? If not, how can one call reincarnation an entirely outmoded notion?

Fifth, all the ancient myths both of immortality and of resurrection seem to be expressible in the myth of reincarnation. As we shall consider in a later chapter, purgatory is strikingly conformable to reincarnationist teaching: the whole process of spiritual evolution can be seen as purgative. I am purged of whatever it was that has bound me to my old karma. The purgation is painful; the release blissful. Yet the bliss cannot be greater than the capacity for bliss that I have attained. Thomas Aquinas, the most influential of the medieval schoolmen, saw that clearly in his own way and dealt with it skillfully. He was confronted by a medieval type of question that we might express as follows: "Heaven is supposed to be a state of perfect happiness; but some people in heaven are the greatest saints who ever lived, while others have only scraped into heaven by the skin of their teeth. If, then, I, being of the latter class, see myself alongside a Francis of Assisi or a Martin of Tours, knowing them to be much holier and therefore happier than I can ever be, how can I be fully happy?" Thomas answered that the beatified in heaven are like cups of various sizes, each cup brimfull, so that even if mine be the smallest cup in heaven it is nevertheless as full as it can be. I am therefore as happy as I can be, and not even Peter or Paul could do better than that. It is like having as much food as you can eat: if, having a small stomach, you have enough to fill it, you are as fully fed as anyone.

Sixth, reincarnationism exalts the individual. In the classic, priestly traditions of the great institutional religions, Brahminical, Jewish and Christian, the emphasis has been on community, covenant, and other such notions that exalt the institution and its functionaries. Buddhism, which became, as did Christianity, a great international religion transcending "blood and soil" ideas and which has always much stressed karmic and other reincarnationist ideas, began as a protest of the individual against institutionalism. My karma is peculiar to *me*. It is *my* problem and the triumph over it is *my* triumph. I may need the help of teachers; I may even profit from my belonging-ness; but in the last resort I am responsible for what I am, as I am becoming responsible for what I shall be. As I struggle through my predicament you may laugh at my antics as you will; but he who laughs last laughs best. In the long run my joy shall be commensurate with the anguish of my present strife. You are seeing an individual in the making, and there is no grander spectacle in all the universe of finite being.

Seventh, and by no means least, reincarnationism takes care of the problem of moral injustice. To the age-old question of Job (why do the wicked prosper and the righteous suffer?) the reincarnationist has a ready answer: we are seeing, in this life, only a fragment of a long story. If you come in at the chapter in which the villain beats the hero to pulp, of course you will ask the old question. You may even put down the book at that point and join forces with those who call life absurd, seeing no justice in the universe. That is because you are too impatient to go on to hear the rest of the story, which will unfold a much richer pattern in which the punishment of the wicked and the vindication of the righteous will be brought to light. Death is but the end of a chapter; it is not, as the nihilists suppose, the end of the story. Yet even now we can already see here and there a glimmer of the process. *Deposuit potentes de sede, et exaltavit humiles:* he has put down the mighty from their seat and has exalted the humble. These joyful words attributed in the *Magnificat* to the Virgin Mary are words we easily understand because, despite our lamentations with Job at the injustice of the world, we have seen in our own brush with human history something of the truth of her joyful proclamation.

Eighth, almost everybody experiences from time to time the sudden and sometimes eerie sense of *déjà vu*, of "having been here before." In a poem entitled *Pre-Existence,* Frances Cornford sees herself lying on the seashore dreaming.

> How all of this had been before;
>   How ages far away
> I lay on some forgotten shore
>   As here I lie today.
>
> The waves came shining up the sands,
>   As here to-day they shine;
> And in my pre-pelasgian hands
>   The sand was warm and fine. [2]

You travel to a distant country whose history and civilization are strikingly alien to your background and education. Suppose you are a Norwegian visiting Turkey or a Finn in Morocco. Suddenly you feel as though long ago you had seen it all before. Some people, having no particular linguistic facility have found that a particular language comes to them as if it were their forgotten maternal tongue, though that is historically impossible in terms of all they know. Suppose you have never been able to make headway in any foreign language, yet when, having gone to Italy, you find Italian comes to you easily, or even, having travelled to India, you suddenly find yourself curiously able to pick up and acquire fluency in Hindi or Tamil. No genetic or historical or sociological explanation satisfactorily accounts for any of these experiences. Attempts at psychological explanation of this *déjà vu* phenomenon seem to be inadequate. Where they resort to a theory such as Jung's "collective unconscious", the presuppositions on which they rely are no more empirically verifiable or falsifiable than are the reincarnational hypotheses they are brought in to replace. While no assent-compelling proof can be offered that these experiences refer to some background from a previous "incarnation", the experiences are peculiarly significant to those who, for other reasons, are disposed to take reincarnationist theory seriously.

The appeal of the myth of reincarnation cuts across race, color and creed, except to the extent that a body of accepted dogma is believed to exclude it. To some extent it also even bridges the gulf between belief and unbelief. Even the least "religious" people find it makes sense, whether they are inclined to believe it or not, while the most thoughtful and sensitive among the "religious" are the least disposed to reject it out of hand.

Such a notion surely merits close inspection, not least since it is conformable to either of two rival, historically important theories about an afterlife. According to one of these main streams in the history of religious ideas, the "essential" part of man, his "ego" or "self" or "soul" is immortal. Unlike the body, which dies like any other animal body, the human soul, being somehow or other of divine origin, perhaps even a spark of the divine fire, is as immortal as is the source of the universe itself. That doctrine, familiar to students of Plato and Plotinus, has influenced Christianity; hence the notion that at death man must go somewhere, be it heaven or hell, for he cannot die. Against this view is another, according to which man has no such entitlement to immortality but may be resurrected to new life. In Christianity this seems clearly to be the Pauline view: man is in a state of sin, and sin normally entails death; nevertheless, through participation in the resurrection of Christ, man can be raised with him to "eternal life".[3] Such a resurrection doctrine, though less commonly associated with reincarnationism than is the other, "immortality" doctrine, might be even more compatible with it. Resurrection is to a new *soma*, a "glorified" body. Why should not this be another incarnation, on this planet or some other far off in outer space? Reincarnation, whatever else it may be, *means* resurrection of some kind. The attainment of a "glorified" body might be through a gradual process.

The fact that the reincarnationist myth can sit with either of these two historic understandings of the nature of human destiny does not mean that either or both must entail it. It does mean that those who reject it should have a good reason for doing so. Closer inspection will reveal that the *theological* reasons usually adduced are too feeble to carry much weight. Too often, indeed, they reflect misunderstanding of the meaning of reincarnational doctrine, the role of karma and the nature of the *samsāra* or chain of rebirths in which the karmic principle issues.

Where reincarnational views are most at home, the presupposition that the soul is independent and akin to the gods is deeply rooted. Convictions of this kind arise understandably at that comparatively primitive level at which human beings become for the first time deeply aware of the miracle of human consciousness. Vedic literature is full of wonderment at what human consciousness can do. In contrast to the rest of animal existence, which is so completely conditioned by and at the mercy of its environment, man can transcend his circumstances. By a miracle I can not only remember a house I saw twenty years ago; I can *imagine* a house I have never seen. There is an echo of this awareness in the punning Spanish couplet:

> *Si la fe es creer lo que no se ve,*
> *Poesía es crear lo que nunca se verá.*

"If faith is believing what you do not see, poetry is creating what you will never see." Poetry, tool of the imagination, can invent mental realities. It can bring into being what never was and never will be in the empirical world.

When this imaginative power is wild it is called, in Italian, *immaginazione*; when it is disciplined and restrained it is called *fantasia*. In English the terms have been reversed: imagination is the restrained lady, fancy her wild sister; but, tamed or wild, creativity of mind is the most godlike power we humans possess. When the ancients first perceived how stupendous is this power and how far it raised them above the animals, they saw in the mind that exercises it an immortal character: that which has such power is imperishable. It is *brahma*.

Paradoxically, we who have learned to use that power so extensively have forgotten what it means to be acutely aware of it. Colin Wilson provocatively suggests: "A man might spend years in prison dreaming of freedom. Yet within twenty-four hours of leaving the jail, he has lost his freedom. The intention he had directed toward freedom has vanished because he is outside the jail. . . . In a paradoxical sense, he was freer in jail."[5] So we have largely lost awareness of the wonder of the power that was so costly to attain. Reincarnationist doctrine, which emerged in humanity when that awareness was at its zenith, calls us back to what it means to have transcended our animal nature and attained awareness of the reality of being a self. That self, whether a spark from beyond the Empyrean imprisoned in mortal flesh or a soul created in the image of him who breathed it into life, is a self that in one way or another participates in the immortality of God that is celebrated in the ancient liturgical acclamation of the Eastern Christian Church: *Hagios ho Theos, Hagios Ischyros, Hagios Athanatos:* Holy God, Holy Strong One, Holy Immortal One.

I shall deal later with what I take to be the most significant scientific objections to reincarnationism. They are not negligible. Even at this preliminary stage of inquiry, however, we may usefully note that reincarnationism is so ill understood that many of the standard objections to it are simply beside the point. Even such a distinguished Cambridge scientist as William Homan Thorpe, for example, in an otherwise admirable book based on his Freemantle Lectures at Balliol, dismisses the whole notion in a single sentence: "And in so far as modern genetical ideas have anything to say upon the subject, they are for mathematical reasons inalterably averse to the concept of reincarnation—the individual's gene complex is unique, never to be precisely repeated in the future of the world."[4] To this the reincarnationist would reply that such uniqueness in the gene complex, far from being incompatible with reincarnationism, is eminently supportive of it. For not only is there no reason why the gene complex should be repeatable; its uniqueness is precisely what, on a karmic view, one would expect. On such a view, what is unique in the story of my spiritual evolution is my karmic need at each rebirth, so of course I must wait (perhaps even for centuries) for just the right combination of genes. The misunderstanding, based on the common notion that reincarnationism is fundamentally a deterministic doctrine when in fact it is the opposite, is widespread. What is remarkable is to find it in such an enlightened animal geneticist so deeply sympathetic to a religious interpretation of evolutionary theory and so perceptive of the need for a marriage of religion and science in our time.

In the contemporary Western scene, reincarnationism, though currently a fashionable topic among both religion-seekers and religion-watchers, is still highly suspect by those who are trained to serious intellectual reflection on religion. Not without reason is it so. Apart from the serious scientific and philosophical objections to it, and irrespective of its ill repute in traditionalist Christian circles, it is often accepted very uncritically, not to say disingenuously, by many people who happen to hit on it and find it an attractive notion. We must also admit that charlatans have taught it. Such facts should not deflect us from our quest. In the Christian Church bishops abound whose every utterance betrays ignorance or turpitude or both; but for all the sadness they lay on the hearts of the more intelligent and perceptive of the faithful, these do not on their account repudiate the apostolic tradition. The fact that some humans lack brains is no argument against thought.

Moreover, one's vision of the afterlife can never be any better or worse than one's vision of God. As Baron von Hügel has perspicaciously observed: "The specifically religious desire of Immortality begins, not with Immortality but with God; it rests upon God; and it ends with God. The religious soul does not seek, find, or assume its own Immortality; and thereupon seek, find, or assume God. But it seeks, finds, experiences, and loves God; and because of God, and of this, its very real, though still very imperfect, intercourse with God . . . it finds, rather than seeks, Immortality of a certain kind."[6] Those whose thought of God is superficial and whose experience of him in their lives casual will always have a correspondingly trivial understanding of the nature of the afterlife in which they profess to believe, be it reincarnational or otherwise. Literalistic Christians, whether calling themselves Protestant or Catholic, have conceived of heaven as a place in the sky, inhabited by harp players and paved with golden streets, with God in the downtown section, replacing City Hall. Such conceptions spring likewise from an impoverished or immature concept of God, to which they are the natural corollary. By the same token, thoughtful Christians need not on their account deny the possibility of an afterlife. As we shall have occasion to notice later in another connection, Lloyd-George, one of the many eminent persons who have expressed belief in reincarnation, once remarked that as a little boy he found heaven an even more terrifying prospect than hell.

In considering the appeal of reincarnationism, we cannot overlook the fact that the standard Christian alternative has entailed the horrific doctrine of hell. That doctrine, that those who are not saved are doomed to eternal punishment, does not seem compatible with the fundamental Christian assertion that God is love. Most of us know enough about the costliness of love to accept the view that all moral progress, like all evolutionary processes, is likely to be painful. We may not boggle, even, at what seems to be the Pauline view that those who fail to win victory with Christ will simply pass out of existence. What is intolerable is the notion that even one sinner should be punished by everlasting torture.

Yet that was in fact both the popular and the official teaching of the medieval Latin Church, inherited by the heirs of the Reformation and for long emphatically preached in both Catholic and Protestant pulpits. True, the learned saw hell as primarily the sense of the eternal loss of the presence of God, the *poena damni;* but in popular understanding it was an unspeakably cruel, fearsome fate. It was represented in medieval and post-medieval art with curiously sadistic persistence. In a thirteenth-century carving in Worcester Cathedral is depicted a damned person who is being roasted over a fire by two devils. The exquisite *Très Riches Heures* of the Duc de Berry portrays Satan spewing up damned souls, which give birth to fiery serpents, which in turn torment them. Lesser devils are engaged in working bellows under a grid. The artist included a large number of priestly victims among the damned, including a bishop who is being dragged by a rope while a devil is screwing a gimlet into his neck with much relish. In the Chapel of St. Brizio in Orvieto Cathedral, a damned woman is depicted as being carried off by a horned and leering devil. Michelangelo's *Last Judgment* in the Sistine Chapel, in which Christ is cursing the lost, is too well-known to need description.

The English Methodist Catechism for 1823, designed for "children of tender years," gives us a fair understanding of the typical Protestant way of instructing the young only last century:

> *Question:* What sort of place is hell?
> *Answer:* A dark and bottomless pit, full of fire and brimstone.

Question: How will the wicked be punished there?
Answer: Their bodies will be tormented with fire, and their
    souls by a sense of the wrath of God.
Question: How long will their torments last?
Answer: The torments of hell will last for ever and ever.

The late G. G. Coulton, a distinguished Cambridge historian, reproduces an Irish Catholic tract by a Redemptorist, which he says was circulating within the lifetime of people still alive when he was writing in 1930.[7] It tells of a child who received sixpence from his father, to buy bread. Instead, the child bought "sugar-sticks and other foolish things." The child had also often neglected the opportunities for grace afforded by the Church: the Mass, the sacraments, prayer, good books. The child dies. The description that follows is not for those with weak stomachs. When the child sees what is happening, it falls down "on its knees before Jesus." It begs for mercy: "Jesus, do not send me to hell. I was a poor ignorant child, I knew no better." Jesus then methodically sets forth the advantages the child has had, and the child is speechless, in fear of the "dreadful sentence" it knows is about to come. "Its heart is bursting with sorrow and anguish." Then comes the awful scene when "Jesus Christ now orders the cross to be taken away. Oh, how the child roars and screams when it sees the cross going away. It is a sign that mercy is no more." The angels and devils are silent. After pronouncing sentence, Jesus Christ lets the devils know that the child now belongs to them. The child now sees the whole sky black with millions of devils. "It cannot get away from them." At last the child is inside hell. It is in a "red-hot oven", burning in agony. "The wicked child has been burning in Hell for years and years. Day and night it has been frightened out of its senses by the terrible cries and groans and howlings of the damned." Then suddenly all hell is silent. A shout like a trumpet goes forth: "Arise, ye dead, and come to judgment." The denizens of hell, including the wicked child, move out to receive the final sentence. They go down again into hell. "The gates of Hell are shut once more and for ever; they will never be opened again! The wicked child is in Hell for ever and ever."[8] The tract is entitled "Books for Children, and Young Persons." It was issued *permissu superiorum* and published by James Duffy and Company, Ltd., 14 and 15 Wellington Quay, Dublin. No date is given; but it probably appeared about 1850.

Now, even allowing for the different climate that prevailed when the tract was published, and for the severe, Jansenist kind of Catholicism the Irish have favored, it is a horrendous testimony to what was acceptable "spiritual reading" for children not so very long ago. The Salvation Army was also strong on hell-fire sermons. Its founder, William Booth, wrote to his future wife in 1854 that people "must have hell-fire flashed before their faces, or they will not move."[9]

It is no wonder that purgatory seemed by comparison, despite its anguish, a demonstration of God's mercy. Purgatory is indeed a far more intelligible concept, in the light of what the Bible says of the nature of God. Even the crassest form of the doctrine of purgatory suggests moral and spiritual evolution. Surely, too, even countless rebirths as a beggar lying in misery and filth on the streets of Calcutta would be infinitely more reconcilable to the Christian concept of God than is the traditional doctrine of everlasting torture in hell. The appeal of reincarnationism to anyone nurtured on hell-fire sermons and tracts is by no means difficult to understand. Indeed, even apart from the notion of everlasting punishment, traditional Christian doctrine about "last things" (the destiny of humankind) is so notoriously confused that vast numbers of people, even habitual churchgoers, have given up believing anything about the subject at all. Christian eschatology (as that branch of theology is called) is by any reckoning the most unsatisfactory area of the Church's concern. A sitting duck for the Church's adversaries, it is also an embarrassment to thoughtful Christians. No wonder, indeed, that the wisest of Christian theologians have discouraged "idle speculation" on the nature of the afterlife. Luther, in his own way, saw the difficulties, and Calvin calls into question his own doctrine of the immortality of the soul, on the ground that Paul intentionally gives no details on the subject, since details "could not help our piety."[10]

REFERENCES AND NOTES

[1]For critique of the objections *see* H. D. Lewis, *The Self and Immortality* (New York: Seabury Press, 1973), and John Hick, *Death and Eternal Life* (London: Collins, 1976). Both of these well-known British philosophers express sympathetic interest in reincarnationism.

[2]*Poems of Today* (London: Sidgwick and Jackson, Ltd., 1918), p. 2.

[3]The difference has been very clearly shown by Oscar Cullmann in a well-known essay. (*See* Bibliography.) Not only do I agree with Cullmann's conclusions on this

subject; I am suggesting a way in which they might be carried much further.

[4]W. H. Thorpe, *Science, Man and Morals* (Ithaca, New York: Cornell University Press, 1966), p. 141.

[5]James F. T. Bugental (ed.), *Challenges of Humanistic Psychology* (New York: McGraw Hill, 1967), p. 6.

[6]F. von Hügel, *Essays and Addresses on the Philosophy of Religion,* Vol. I (New York: Dutton, 1924 and 1926), p. 197.

[7]J. Furniss, C.SS.R., "The Terrible Judgment and the Bad Child". In G. G. Coulton, *Romanism and Truth,* Vol. I (London: Faith Press, 1930), Appendix VI, p. 145.

[8]Coulton, *Romanism and Truth,* p. 147.

[9]H. Begbie, *Life of William Booth* Vol. I (London: Macmillan, 1920), p. 228.

[10]J. Calvin, on 1 Cor.: 13.12. In *Corpus Reformatorum,* 77, 515. Cf. *Institutes,* III, 25, 6.

II

IS REINCARNATION COMPATIBLE WITH CHRISTIAN FAITH?

Many times man lives and dies
Within his two eternities,
That of race and that of soul,
And ancient Ireland knew it all.

W. B. Yeats, *Under Ben Bulben*

Is reincarnation compatible with Christian faith? Before even seeking an answer to that question, we had better consider whether it is a good question. If, moreover, it is a good question, to whom is it important?

The notion of reincarnation, we have seen, is both widespread in the history of religion and extraordinarily persistent in the literature of the world. Besides, it is exercising renewed influence on the minds of thoughtful men and women today, not least on younger people. Most people assume that, even apart from the philosophical and scientific objections to which a later chapter is to be devoted, reincarnation is a notion so alien to the central tradition of the Christian Church, and so contrary to the Bible, that it could not be entertained within the structure of even the most liberal, not to say easygoing, interpretation of Christian faith. The assumption is natural and seems *prima facie* justified. The notion of reincarnation, with the concept of karma that attends all the developed

14

forms of it that are worthy of consideration by civilized human beings, must be said to be generally associated with oriental forms of religion that are profoundly alien to what historians commonly call the great monotheistic faiths: Judaism, Christianity, and Islam. These faiths, which all stress the concept of God as the One who acts in history, are in important respects so different from religions such as Buddhism and its Hindu parent that it seems at first sight unlikely that a doctrine so peculiarly associated with one group should be assimilable by the other. When, therefore, people in the West, who, in so far as they have any religious allegiance at all, are usually Christians or Jews, are attracted to reincarnationist ideas, they tend to think they have to make a choice. Either they accept the Bible as containing in some sense the Word of God, in which case they cannot honestly flirt with reincarnationist notions, or else they renounce the uniqueness of the Bible, relegating it to a mere place among the religious literatures of mankind, and perhaps not a particularly important place at that. If they are Christians, they will also be likely to feel that either they must confess the apostolic faith as set forth in the ancient creeds, and live the Gospel as best they can within the Household of Faith that is the Church, being sustained therein by the sacraments (in which case they think they must renounce reincarnationism as untenable), or else they must abandon their Christian heritage.

It may be, indeed, that reincarnationism is simply not a viable option for a Christian. It may even be that it is, as some think, a pernicious occult teaching that is a snare for those who would walk the Christian Way. Certainly, it is often accounted at least a strange deviation for a Christian, if it be nothing worse. No less noteworthy is the fact that such a view of the matter is by no means a recent development. There is no doubt that in Western Christendom, at any rate, the myth of reincarnation would have seemed as strange to a medieval Catholic theologian such as Anselm or Thomas Aquinas as it would have appeared to Luther or Calvin, or to the average Christian today, whether he dub himself Protestant or Catholic. Yet an examination of the history of Christian thought, in the light of the very complex issues that emerge through the application of modern scholarly methods, suggests that the answer to the question is likely to be much less decisive. Cardinal Mercier is among those who, in modern times, have opined that reincarnationism has never been formally condemned by the Roman Catholic Church.[1]

Nicolas Berdyaev, a highly original Christian thinker whose Russian Orthodox background gives his thought on such matters a different dimension from that of most Western thinkers, has many interesting things to say on death and immortality. "Victory over death," he writes, "is not the last and final victory. Victory over death is too much concerned with time. The last, final and ultimate victory is victory over hell."[2] After alluding to the injustice of the traditional notion of hell in which people are tormented eternally for "sins committed in time," he goes on to note: "There is more justice in the doctrine of Karma and reincarnation, according to which deeds done in time are expiated in time and not in eternity, and man has other and wider experience than that between birth and death in this one life." But then he goes on to affirm roundly: "Theosophical theory of reincarnation cannot be accepted by the Christian mind." After so saying, however, he points out at once: "But it is essential to recognize that man's final fate can only be settled after an infinitely greater experience in spiritual worlds than is possible in our short earthly life."[3] If this be so, as seems to me an inescapable conclusion for Christians and one supported by the long and ancient tradition of an "intermediate state", why the rejection out of hand of reincarnationism as something quite unacceptable "by the Christian mind"?

The Bible does not explicitly teach reincarnationism. That is to say, there is no pronouncement on the subject, either in the Old Testament or in the New, to which one could point and by means of it compel the acceptance of a person who felt bound to receive as divine revelation everything that is clearly and unequivocally affirmed in Holy Scripture. No *such* biblical warrant for reincarnation exists.

That, however, does not take us far, since much the same could be said of the doctrine of the Trinity, which is surely held to be a classic expression of orthodox Christian belief about God. Except for the text in the first letter of John (1 John 5.7), known to scholars to be a very late interpolation, no direct biblical warrant exists for the doctrine of the Trinity as formulated by the Church.[4] That absence of direct biblical warrant for the doctrine of the Trinity does not mean, however, that the trinitarian formula is antipathetic to the teaching of the New Testament writers. On the contrary, it was held to be, and within Christian orthodoxy it has continued to be accounted, a proper formulation of a great truth about God that is implicit in New Testament teaching. There is no reason at all why the doctrine of reincarnation *might* not be in a similar case. Whether it is so in fact remains to be seen. As we shall see, there is remarkable support for it in Scripture, in the Fathers, and in later Christian literature. There are also serious philosophical and theological difficulties.

From a Christian standpoint, the most fundamental objection to reincarnationism, as commonly presented, is the notion that man is a part of God, a spark of the divine. According to Christian teaching, and true to the Jewish heritage in Christianity, man is made in the image of God, yet he is no more than an image. He is a creation of God, not an emanation. All attempts at blurring this distinction have been vigorously resisted, for they are evidences of a failure to understand what the Bible says about the human condition, its grandeur in having God as its creator and its limitation in being nevertheless a fallen creature. In Judaism and Islam, the gulf between God and man is such that the notion of the Incarnation of God in Christ is blasphemous and therefore abhorrent. In Islam, *shirk* (idolatry, the association of any creature with God) has always been the supreme sin. Christianity is deeply sympathetic to that concern, for it shares with Judaism and Islam a profound awareness of the gulf between the human and the divine; nevertheless, it proclaims the supreme paradox of the Christian faith: God bridged that gulf in the Person of Christ. The gulf, however, remains. In recognizing the gulf, Christianity is at one with Judaism and Islam.

The typical Hindu teaching is quite different. It is shared, moreover, by many other systems, such as various forms of Buddhism in the East and, in the West, Stoicism and Neoplatonism. There man is seen as an emanation of God, not a creation. Characteristic of much Hindu teaching on this subject is the view that God has two modes of being, a substantive and an emanating one. The whole cosmos, as the emanation of God, may be called an extension of the divine being. The human soul manifests in a special way this God-like nature of all things. The highly developed soul, the spiritual leader or prophet or saint, manifests God more clearly still. From there it is very easy to go on to recognize *avatars* of deity as illustrious examples of such a manifestation, much as one might recognize Plato and Kant and Spinoza as more than ordinarily great figures in the history of human thought and, similarly, Planck and Einstein as very special giants in modern science. Jesus would be certainly a great *avatar* of deity; but neither he nor any other "holy man" or prophet, however eminent in spirituality, could ever be properly called (as Christians call Jesus Christ) radically different from all others such as Gotama and Shankara and Moses, all of whom are high on the scale of holiness. To the Hindu mind, to say that Jesus Christ is so to be distinguished would be like saying that Einstein is not merely one of the greatest geniuses in the history of science but is fundamentally and qualitatively different from all other men of science who ever have existed and ever could exist. Plainly, not even the most ardent admirer of Einstein would claim that. Indeed, he would probably be the first to laugh at it. Yet that is precisely the claim Christians make about Jesus Christ.

The type of attitude we have been considering as typical of Hinduism and Neoplatonism springs from a presupposition that every human being is essentially divine, as every biological entity is essentially endowed with life: the difference between a jellyfish and a horse is only a matter of degree in the manifestation of divinity. Now, it is true that reincarnationism is historically much associated with that presupposition and the attitudes that it engenders. It does not follow, however, that reincarnationist notions are inseparable from these attitudes.

Given that presupposition, the seeker believes he has a clear vision of the purpose of human life and, if he is willing to work at his beliefs, he will try to realize his identity with the divine, for that is, on his view, the way to advance his spirituality. In Hindu language, the purpose of life is to realize the complete identity of *ātman* (the God-who-is-within-me) with *brahman* (the God-who-is-the-Absolute). So close is the connection in Indian thought that the achievement of this unity has a name: it is called *brahman-ātman*.

When we ask, as naturally we must, how *ātman* ever came to be so separated from *brahman* as to call for efforts toward that achievement, we get an answer that is in itself not very different from the Christian answer: the individual has fallen into an estrangement from his proper condition. For the Christian, the estrangement consists in the failure of fallen humanity to acknowledge and delight in its creaturely relationship to its Creator. The essence of this "original" sin is pride. In the Hebrew creation myth, the serpent in the Garden of Eden successfully tempted Eve by pointing out to her that the reason God had forbidden the tree in the middle of the garden was that God knew very well that if she and her husband ate it they would be "like gods",[5] For the Hindu and other emanationists, humanity has been estranged from its proper condition, not through an arrogant and futile attempt at identification with God but, on the contrary, through a failure to recognize as reality that very identification with God that the biblical tradition accounts illusory and fundamentally evil, an aim that is to be above all avoided by those who would put themselves in the right way. At this point, then, the two understandings of man's relationship to God are diametrically opposed. Moreover, there is no doubt that, historically, reincarnationist views are associated with the Hindu type of understanding rather than with the orthodox Jewish and Christian one.

According to the emanationist view, the model we are to have in mind is that of the soul entrapped and enmeshed in a distorted, warped vision of reality. Instead of seeing the cosmic state of affairs as it is, plainly, as if through still, clear water, the soul sees it distorted, as fractured through a troubled, muddy, sea. This spiritual astigmatism is due to enslavement to what Hindu literature calls *māyā,* a Sanskrit term signifying a condition into which all manifestations of the divine fall in the very act of becoming manifest. It might be conceptualized as a sort of cloud that accompanies the divine wherever the divine manifests itself, shrouding it in such a way as to give the illusion of a reality different from the only reality there is: the divine.

Now, *this* view, unlike the view that presupposes identification with the divine as humanity's true goal, is not *entirely* alien to Christian tradition. Christianity inherited something like it, not only through the channels of early Christian modes of thought in the Gentile world, but also through biblical and intertestamental Judaism, which was already much influenced by Greek ideas in the centuries immediately preceding the birth of Jesus. Moreover, Christianity, when influenced by this view, can also be hospitable to reincarnationism, because then it can encourage the notion that for the soul to find its way back to a proper vision of reality and a right relationship to it, we must expect a long evolutionary, purgatorial process. The task is not only too complex and too arduous to be quickly accomplished; it is of such a nature that set-backs are to be expected. When a man is waist-deep in slimy mud and struggling manfully to extricate himself from it, he may sometimes seem to be slipping back two feet for every foot he advances. Salvation, however quickly assured (as some Christians believe it to be) is not quickly achieved. The rescue operation, even with the help of those life belts thrown to the endangered soul (the "amazing grace" and "bountiful providence" that Christians joyfully acknowledge), is likely to take a long time. "Heaven is not winne with a wish," as the seventeenth century Zachary Boyd quaintly writes in *The Last Battell of the Soul*, a treatise of the soul's struggle with the forces of evil that seek to engulf and stifle it. The soul's progress is not to be seen in a small slice; we must look at the whole graph.

In all this the emanationist view, as exemplified in Hindu lore, and the creationist one, as presented in the Bible, do not radically conflict, as do their respective presuppositions about the aim of the redemptive process. Why, then, might not reincarnation be assimilated by Christians as part of their faith? Though orthodox Christians could not accept the typical Hindu view of the aim of the spiritual life, they can agree, at least in some measure, on its nature and the difficulties attending it. Might not the Indian notion of the inexorable spiritual law of *karma,* which governs all moral action and spiritual endeavor, be adapted to the Christian outlook? Might not an orthodox Christian see the *samsāra* or chain of incarnations, of which we hear so much in Hindu lore, as the most satisfactory way in which to conceptualize the journey of the soul to the state that Christians traditionally call heaven or the Beatific Vision, in which the soul at last is so completely purified that it can stand in the right relation to God and, as the old Scottish Catechism promises, "enjoy Him for ever"? At first sight, at any rate, it would now seem that Christians, far from resisting reincarnationism as an exotic, alien idea, should be ready to embrace it as one that might both enlighten their minds and add a new and exhilarating dimension to their faith.

That is not to say, of course, that a Christian could ever honestly take over all the paraphernalia of oriental presuppositions. Still less does it entitle him to select uncritically, from a variety of ideas in Hinduism and other traditions, those that happen to please his fancy. Such eclecticism is not by any reckoning allowable to an honest man. Even the most elementary acquaintance with Christian history would show us that the Church had to face such dangers in its early days and, but for resistance to the temptation to become a general repository for all religious ideas that came its way, would have been swallowed up in the general Mediterranean melting-pot. Nevertheless, as we shall see, the notion of rebirth was so widespread in the primitive Church that the answer to our question may turn out to be more ambiguous than seemed to be at first likely. Moreover, resurrection was, of course, a fundamental part of the Christian *kerygma,* the message of salvation, that the early Christian apostles proclaimed, and its exact nature is never specified. We shall find, too, that although, for various historical reasons, reincarnationist ideas fell out of favor and came to be associated with sects that were far removed, by any reckoning, from the Christian Way, they have also been entertained by eminently responsible thinkers committed to the ancient Catholic faith. They have also been very widely held by great men and women in the profoundly religious kind of humanist tradition that goes back to Socrates and flourished in the Quattrocento and later.

Even the popularly held notion that the doctrine of reincarnation is peculiar to India is, of course, erroneous. The doctrine is so widespread that India cannot even be said to be its cradle. The Indus Valley, through a very great focus and clearing-house of religious ideas, is by no means the only source of the reincarnationist theme. Reincarnation occurs in many forms, some crude, some highly sophisticated and profoundly ethical. In crude forms it appears in many societies. Sir James Frazer reported long ago that the Eskimos around the Bering Strait believe that the souls of dead sea-beasts, such as seals and whales, are reincarnated in fresh bodies. He also mentions that the Kwakiutl Indians of British Columbia think that when a salmon is killed its soul returns to the salmon country, so "they take care to throw the bones and offal into the sea, in order that the soul may reanimate them at the resurrection of the salmon."[6] No doubt India has been more deeply affected by reincarnationist concepts than has been any other surviving civilization and Indian thought has developed the notion along very noble lines, but other civilizations have also independently developed forms of reincarnationist belief, including, of course, Plato's mythological heritage of it from Pythagoras.

Reincarnation is known in the history of religion under several names: transmigration, rebirth, metempsychosis. These terms are sometimes used synonymously by historians of religion. Sometimes one term is used in opposition to another. Modern theosophists, for example, generally prefer to reserve the term "metempsychosis" for the more primitive, magical forms of the doctrine that envision movement from a human to a bestial existence, and they use the term "reincarnation" of the more developed, ethical forms of the doctrine, such as are found, for instance, in their own view and have played such a fundamental role in Mahayana Buddhism. For the purpose of our present study we need not be much concerned with making that distinction, since we are presupposing, of course, an ethical and karmic form of the doctrine. Within the Christian tradition of "resurrection", the term *metensomatosis*, used by Clement of Alexandria, might be accounted more accurate for Christian use; but since it would seem pedantic I shall use it only in special contexts and shall adopt no special vocabulary for distinguishing forms of reincarnationist theory. The term "reincarnation" often implies, for instance, the mind-matter dualism of the Gnostics; but it need not do so. The term "pre-existence", however, may sometimes have to be used distinctively, since it refers to a particular doctrine in the history of Christian thought that may but does not necessarily encompass the notion of reincarnation.

The widespread notion that Christianity must wholly exclude all forms of reincarnationism is very understandable. It has never been officially entertained by the Church, has sometimes been officially frowned on, and has generally been at least suspect. Nevertheless, the supposition that there is a clear, unambiguous biblical or patristic or conciliar teaching about immortality and resurrection would be mistaken. On the contrary, though the expectation of an afterlife is certainly an integral part of Christian faith and constitutes Christian hope, its form is far less clearly defined than is popularly supposed. True, heaven and hell have been seen as alternative destinies for the good and the wicked respectively, and within central Christian traditions, Greek, Roman and Anglican, purgatory has also played a role as a key concept. Nevertheless, attempts to say anything specific about these states have often, if not generally, ended in intellectual confusion, not to say disaster. The wisest of theologians have tended to be reticent about detailing the celestial and infernal geographies.

Dante, in the greatest Christian epic of all time, drew a vivid picture of all three (hell, purgatory and paradise), in the earthy terms in which the medieval mind loved to clothe its most ineffable ideas. So precise and definite is he that with modern technology any geographer today ought to be able to discover the exact location of the Gates of Hell and find his way to the mountain slopes of purgatory, if only he could be literalistic enough to pursue such a quest. Since Dante places the various heavens on known astronomical bodies, with the moon as the site of the lowest heaven, we may hope to make excursions thither and back in the foreseeable future. Of course Dante's very poetic precision is possible for him only because he, like his contemporaries, were so accustomed to allegorizing that they could afford the use of concrete images of the kind in which he delights. No educated, thoughtful person could ever be misled into taking such images literally, either in Dante's day or in our own. When it comes to theological definition, the less said about the exact nature of our final destiny the better. So heaven becomes simply the clear vision of God, hell the final loss of that vision, and purgatory the intermediate state of purification.

Yet of course, as we shall abundantly see, there are other considerations. The attitude of people toward the notion of an afterlife is governed by a wide variety of presuppositions, especially their understanding of the nature of God. Christianity has inherited a long tradition on that subject, both from the Bible and from the thought of the Gentile world that moulded the intellectual form of Christian belief from the first century onwards. So despite the deliberate vagueness and salutary ambiguity among theologians that has often been a welcome relief from the hell-fire sermons and pearly-gate promises in which popular preachers have from time to time indulged, Christians have generally geared their vision of the afterlife to their understanding of the nature of God. One cannot overestimate the importance of the truth that our vision of the future life is a corollary of our concept of God. We must also not overlook and should not underestimate the difference between the Christian understanding and the thought of, say, impersonalistic Vedanta. The Christian mode of conceptualizing God, rooted in its Jewish heritage, and therefore uncompromisingly monotheistic, is very different indeed from that of the pantheism characteristic of much Hindu and Buddhist thought. That difference is reflected in the respective attitudes to the destiny of man. The latitude available to Christians within the structure of their faith may turn out to be, therefore, less hospitable to reincarnationism than some might hope and others fear. Any sanguine hopes we may harbor for bringing such ideas within the Christian Household of Faith should be tempered with caution.

When all that is said, however, we should also be prepared for surprises in the other direction. The hospitality of the Christian Way to reincarnationist notions may turn out to be greater than we may have believed possible. Certainly they appear unexpectedly and persistently in the history of Christian thought. The hostility they have encountered cannot easily be shown to have any profound philosophical or theological justification undergirding it. On the contrary, it sometimes suggests trivial or unworthy causes, such as ignorance, prejudice, intellectual confusion, or fear. Political fears have too often inhibited theological development. Notoriously, religious prejudices often arise for very superficial reasons. One has only to think of the long-standing prejudice in the Roman Catholic Church against cremation, which many no doubt took to have some theological basis but which originated, like so many other human prejudices, by a sort of guilt by association: pagans cremated their dead, so Christians should do otherwise. It is true, of course, that the doctrine of the resurrection of the body is likely to have made cremation repugnant to many Christians from early times; but there could have been no well-considered theological objection to it, since it does what burial does, only more quickly and efficiently. That reincarnationist doctrine may have been in a similar case is a possibility we should bear in mind as our study proceeds.

No honest Christian could be *entirely content* with the Hindu or Buddhist understanding of the religious situation of mankind. For these great Asiatic religions, which have been rightly called "religions of eternal cosmic law," imply a state of affairs that orthodox Christians have always believed to be that which Jesus Christ came to end. There is truth in the slogan of some modern theologians that Christianity is not a religion but the end of religions. That is, indeed, precisely what the primitive Church saw behind the Death and Resurrection of Christ. The apostolic teaching was and is that the old rites are done away and the old bonds broken. So there is a dimension in the Christian faith that no karmic principle or reincarnationist doctrine could fully contain, since Jesus Christ is held to be victorious over the very state of affairs they represent. Karma is the Indian expression of belief in a moral order in the cosmos. Whatever Christian teaching is, it certainly goes beyond the limits of any moral order we could conceive.

Nevertheless, it does not purport to destroy that order. In the culture into which Jesus was born, the Torah was the expression of such a moral order. It was the Law of God delivered to Moses and set forth in the first five books of the Bible. Second only to the Torah in importance was another part of the Bible, known as "the

Prophets.'' In the Sermon on the Mount, Jesus is reported as expressly telling his hearers: "Do not imagine that I have come to abolish the Law or the Prophets. I have not come to abolish but to complete."[7] By the same token, the karmic law that is an oriental expression of the cosmic moral order is not to be accounted subject to abolition by the Gospel, only to completion.

In the midst of the German Enlightenment in the eighteenth century, Kant gave the West a concept of duty that is based on the notion of a moral order not radically different from that which lies behind karmic doctrine, allowing, of course, for great differences in cultural expression. Kant deeply influenced many Christians in the nineteenth century, and his influence has not by any means entirely eroded. Many educated Christians today would not boggle at writing "Duty" for "Law" in the context to which we have just referred. Jesus does not come to abolish Duty but to complete it. Why, then, might not Christians speak of "Karma and the Gospel" with a similar relationship in mind? We shall return to this Kantian theme in a later chapter devoted to the notion of moral evolution.

From the time of Justin Martyr in the first century, who was, by the way, an early Christian reincarnationist, Christians have been ready to express themselves in the categories of Gentile thought. The doctrine of the Trinity, which was finally formulated a few centuries later, is a celebrated example of that accommodation to an idiom alien to the culture out of which Christianity emerged. The presuppositions underlying the doctrine of karma are more intelligible to many Christians today than those undergirding the venerable and beautiful doctrine of the Trinity have been for a long time. It is unlikely, indeed, that the underpinnings of the doctrine of the Trinity will be ever again intelligible to any but a comparatively small group of Hellenistic scholars. (After all, even the Latin world, at the time the doctrine was so skillfully devised, did not really understand it, as modern scholars now see very well.) The notion of reincarnation, with the karmic doctrine underlying and morally justifying it, is by comparison easy for anyone to grasp who is in the least inclined to think in any sort of religious terms. If, then, one could show that there is as much truth in it as in, say, the biblical Torah, might not it conceivably play a role in Christian thought at least similar to that extremely important role that the Torah, the Law of Moses, has played from New Testament times onwards in the thought and lives of Christians?

Contrary to a popular misunderstanding in the West, the doctrine of karma does not eliminate or even diminish human freedom. It is no more a determinism than is the Torah. Of course it entails a deterministic aspect; but so do all doctrines of human freedom, as every student of twentieth century existentialism knows. If there be any sense at all in talking of human freedom, it can only be within the context of some pattern of determinism. I can no more exercise freedom in a vacuum than I can escape from a prison that is not there. So of course the karma I am constantly making for myself operates according to a cosmic law that is a foil to my freedom; nevertheless, it is I who make it. Nowhere could there be a notion that more patently entails that of moral responsibility. It is indeed precisely on that account that it *can* be interpreted in such a way as to expose the doctrine of karma to the objection that it engenders a salvation-by-works outlook that would not measure up to what orthodox Christians, especially in the Pauline and Augustinian teaching, account the Gospel of Grace. That is no more reason to repudiate it, however, than the Gospel is a reason to renounce the Ten Commandments or, for that matter, the summary of the Law: "Thou shalt love the Lord with all thy heart . . . and thy neighbor as thyself."[8]

I am not asking the reader to make up his mind in advance about the question I have put before him in this chapter. I ask only that he open his mind to an important and interesting possibility. As we conduct our inquiry we must see, each one for himself, what the evidence warrants.

REFERENCES AND NOTES

[1] See Bibliography: Spencer, Frederick A. M. Roman Catholics will also note that no papal encyclical against reincarnation has been issued.

[2] N. Berdyaev, *The Destiny of Man* (London: Geoffrey Bles, 1937), p. 336.

[3] Ibid., p. 349.

[4] "For there are three that bear record in heaven, the Father, the Word, and the Holy Ghost; and these three are one." (K.J.V.) These words, not found in any independent Greek text, or in the Old Latin versions or the Vulgate as issued by Jerome, are omitted from scholarly modern translations such as the Jerusalem Bible, the New English Bible, and the Revised Standard Version.

[5] Genesis:3.4.

[6] J. G. Frazer, *The Golden Bough* (abridged edition) (New York: Macmillan Company, 1930), p. 526.

[7] Matthew:5.17 (J.B.)

[8] Matthew:22.37-40; cf. Deuteronomy:6.5; Leviticus:19.18.

III

SOME INTERPRETATIVE CONSIDERATIONS

> *The soul . . . if immortal, existed before our birth, and if the former existence no-ways concerns us, neither will the latter. . . . The Metempsychosis is, there-fore, the only system of this kind that phi-losophy can hearken to.*
>
> David Hume, *Essay on the Immortality of the Soul*

Reincarnationism is usually associated with certain life styles and thought patterns that are more typical of the Orient than of the West. Of course, in vast civilizations such as those of India and China no one outlook has ever totally prevailed; nevertheless, a disposition that seems to have found a favorable soil in India and that has spread thence to other parts of the Orient has tended to engender the view that life is to be regarded as a burden, even as a punishment, rather than as a favor or grace. To be rid of life is therefore a boon rather than a catastrophe. No doubt the average person in such societies has not so looked on life; but under the influence of the leaders of thought they have come to associate such an outlook with wisdom. To the extent that they have given any thought at all to the mysteries of existence, they have tended to follow that lead, admiring those who downgrade life. In a militaris-tic society a man may feel personally no stomach for battle; but he

27

is conditioned to applaud military glory and to admire soldiery as heroism, as people in economically-vigorous industrial societies have tended to admire business enterprise and applaud the successful tycoon. So while the average American has generally admired the rags-to-riches millionaire, the average Indian has been ready to revere the man who leaves family and home to wander forth with his begging bowl as a sannyasi.

In such a moral climate the *samsāra* or chain of rebirth is generally accounted a misery from which we naturally hope to escape. Karma is the reality from which religion is expected to free us. The goal is to go beyond it to nirvana and so have done with it for ever. In the West, on the contrary, our view of life is less pessimistic. For all the tragedy attending life, it is intrinsically good. It needs only to be made better. Christ, in providing for its gradual but infinite betterment, has indeed redeemed the world, which without him is doomed to everlasting slavery. For the Christian, human life is to be transformed rather than terminated.

The effect of that radical difference of approach to human life on our interpretation of reincarnation is inevitably profound. While the typical oriental reincarnationist is studying to free himself from the chain of rebirth that is imposed upon him by his karma and that cannot be avoided till his karma is worked out, the occidental reincarnationist is looking to ways of improving his karma so that rebirth will bring him a richer, fuller life. So when reincarnationism has come to the West in the form of esoteric knowledge from the East, distilled out of an imported Buddhism, it has generally seemed to be in fundamental opposition to the presuppositions of the culture to which it has addressed itself. To say that is not to say that these oriental presuppositions are false. It is to say, however, that they are separable from whatever truth there may be in re-incarnationism.

No concept in the history of religious ideas is more confused than is that of immortality. Not only does it take many different forms; the forms it takes are based on presuppositions about the nature of life and death, man and God, that are in some cases radically opposed.

In the New Testament, for instance, we get no unambiguous statement of what precisely the promise of eternal life is supposed to accomplish. If the soul is perishable, presumably eternal life is a gift that saves it from annihilation. If the soul is imperishable, what does eternal life add? According to one element in early Christian thought on the subject, the soul of man, having come from God (whether as a spark of the divine fire, as Stoic tradition would have it, or from the in-breathing of God's *ruach* into the dust for the creation of man, as is one of the biblical forms of the myth), is in its nature immortal. That is why, after the death of the body, it must live on, whether in another body or in a disembodied state, whether in another life on earth or in heaven or purgatory or hell. There is, however, a very different view that finds expression in the letters of Paul and elsewhere, according to which the soul has no such separate status.

This view seems to accord with the more indigenous of the alternatives then prevailing in Jewish tradition, according to which man is a unity, body and soul. What touches one touches the other: the one cannot exist without the other. So man's "natural" destiny is the grave; but because of the resurrection of Christ (such is Pauline teaching) a man may be endowed with a new and miraculous capacity: through Christ he may "win the victory" over death and so rise in a glorified body (*soma*) to "eternal life". In the Apocalypse, the 144,000 stand in white robes and with the palms of victory in their hands. These and other notions are found interwoven in Christian thought, including, as we shall see, theories of the pre-existence of the soul and other expressions of the ancient myth of reincarnation.

The issue has been usefully discussed in recent times by a number of writers among whom may be mentioned Professors Oscar Cullmann, Jaroslav Pelikan and Helmut Thielicke.[1] Pelikan's conclusion is a characteristic one in the Christian tradition: "The core of the Christian faith is pessimism about life and optimism about God and therefore hope for life in God."[2] One is reminded of Whittier's lines, which John Baillie used to quote approvingly:

> *I know not where His islands lift*
> *Their fronded palms in air;*
> *I only know I cannot drift*
> *Beyond His love and care.*[3]

Thielicke is much more emphatic and dogmatic in his denunciation of what he calls "secular" theories of immortality, which he takes to have vitiated much Christian thinking too, including of course all reincarnationist teaching.[4] These he roundly calls blasphemous. He even calls one understanding of the notion, as he

sees it to have entered the Catholic tradition, "the ultimate refinement of blasphemy for it sets God in analogy to man."[5]

The point such writers are making is an important one for such as
take seriously the Christian promise of resurrection. The notion
that this promise is radically incompatible with reincarnationist
and other widespread and traditional doctrines in the history of
religions is much less clear. Thielicke's view represents a particular strain in Christian tradition, the one of which Tertullian is a
classic spokesman: "What has Athens to do with Jerusalem?"
There is another strain in Christian thought, however, in which the
humanist and Christian traditions are seen, not as mutually irrelevant and hostile camps but as mutually supportive. That approach
need do nothing, in my judgment, to diminish the force or wonder
of the Christian *kerygma* or detract from its particularity. On the
contrary, those who most value that hope should find that the
humanist tradition and the various immortality and reincarnationist theories it encompasses enhance rather than diminish the particular grandeur of the Christian hope.

To be sure, the myth of reincarnation is bound up with certain
presuppositions about the nature of man. For example, the soul
cannot be understood to move from one body to another unless it is
conceived as having in some way or other an independent existence. Contemporary empiricist philosophers find such a notion
unintelligible; but it has played such an enormously important role
in the history of religious ideas that before discarding it we must try
to make sense of it if we can. The concept of human life as a
pilgrimage would seem to be as characteristic of Buddhist as of
Christian thought, though of course the *nature* of the pilgrimage
may be variously conceived. Indeed it is variously conceived
within Buddhism and also within Christianity. The presuppositions of reincarnationism need not be, however, as totally disconnected with the Christian hope as Thielicke insists. True,
Christian orthodoxy, following the whole biblical tradition, insists
in a peculiar way on the almightiness of God and on man's total
dependence on the divine initiative. That emphasis is not characteristic of the oriental way of symbolizing concepts of immortality
and reincarnation. Nevertheless, we must notice that the *remedies*
respectively claimed could be variously conceived, though the
circumstances that call for these remedies might not be radically
different. We should bear this point in mind as we look at reincarnation and its presuppositions.

We have seen that the notion of human rebirth is extremely ancient and remarkably widespread, that in the history of religions it has taken many different forms and has been very diversely interpreted, and that it has appeared under various names: re-incarnation, transmigration, rebirth, metempsychosis. Though it is much associated with India and those Asiatic cultures that have been nourished by the thought of that great vortex of religious engagement and reflection, anthropologists have found it in primitive, animistic religion in places as remote from each other as Africa and Lapland.

Anthropologists have found, for example, that the Lapps are among those who hold that the spirit of a deceased ancestor who is about to be incarnated in a child instructs the pregnant mother in a dream how her child is to be named. Similar expectations have been found to occur among the American Koloshes. Some African negroes, astonished at the deathly color of the white men they first encountered, have propounded the theory that their own dead must have returned in a strange, pallid form.

If reincarnation in its classic form is to be an intelligible notion, belief that the soul is capable of movement in and out of a body must be presupposed. The typical primitive belief that the soul, being apparently conceived as quasi-material, can slip out through the nostrils at death (or even on the point of a spear, when the death is a violent one) gives rise to various superstitions such as one against sleeping with the mouth open. A modern survival of this superstition is found in the practice of saying *Gesundheit* (health, soundness) to the victim of a sneeze: the function of the magic formula is to keep the soul in the body in which it is currently incarnate. All such notions plainly enough reflect a belief that souls are capable of existence apart from a body; but they are also very hospitable to the hardly less widespread belief that they are nevertheless somehow ill at ease in a disembodied state and are therefore always on the lookout for a bodily habitation. Associated with the belief are practices such as one found among Greenlanders of emptying an igloo before they leave it uninhabited: the belief of these people is that Torngarsuk, a rapacious deity, is always on the lookout for uninhabited dwellings and, if one is comfortably equipped, he will take up house in it as a squatter who will be difficult to dislodge.

The connection between such ideas and the more primitive forms of transmigrationist theory, in which human souls can be reincarnated in animals and even in trees, is easily seen. The process by which more developed forms of reincarnationism take shape is perhaps less obvious; yet it is really no more remarkable than are other developments in the history of religion, such as the development in classical Judaism of an ethical type of religion and its gradual triumph over more ancient and primitive cultic ancestors. The form in which reincarnationist doctrine is usually presented to students of religion is the one associated with many forms of Hinduism and Buddhism, in which the chain of incarnations (*samsāra*) is governed by an impersonal moral law, the law of *karma,* which determines that ethical acts are rewarded by conditions favorable for spiritual advancement, while unethical acts have negative consequences that put impediments in the way of those who have perpetrated them. Where this understanding of reincarnationism prevails, it is accompanied by strong emphasis on moral freedom. Western critics of the doctrine have commonly attributed to it certain objectionable consequences, such as a moral procrastination that would be a trans-incarnational form of the still unconverted Augustine's celebrated youthful prayer "Give me chastity but not yet."—or else a moral paralysis that expresses itself in fatalism and a "no-use-fighting-my-karma" posture. Such attitudes are quite alien to the thought of India. Of course people in India have sometimes exhibited them; but in doing so they have done no better justice to karmic theory than did those of Cromwell's soldiers who went forth to battle with bible and sword, certain that the Lord would have to be on their side, no matter what they did, do justice to the Calvinistic doctrine of blessed assurance. A theological doctrine is not to be judged by what we see among those who parody it.

Reincarnationism does not seem to have been universal even in India. Though Radhakrishnan, an eminent Hindu scholar, sees it even in the *Rig-Veda,* the earliest of the *Vedas* that constitute India's most ancient literature, most Western scholars have generally seen little if any reincarnationism in the *Vedas*.[6] The *Rig-Veda* certainly does not present, to say the least, any full-blown account in reincarnationist terms. It teaches, rather, a doctrine of immortality in a paradise with the gods. At any rate, we must assume that reincarnation was not part of the general presuppositions of *all* ancient Indian religion, since according to a reference in the *Upanishads* centuries later (by which time the notion had come to be well recognized), neither Śvetaketu nor his father, Gautama, had heard of it. The reason given is that it was a doctrine of the military class, the kshatriyas, and was then for the first time disclosed to a brahmin.[7] Such an admission suggests that the brahmins, the learned or priestly caste, recognize the reincarnation myth as one of those having roots in the past: it is one myth among many. It is one, however, that the brahmins adopted and, in their own way, rationalized by giving it ethical and metaphysical formulation. Their function *in this respect* was not entirely unlike that of the Hebrew prophets who took the old primitive concept of Yahweh and invested it with the new dignity of Yahweh Sabaoth, the Lord of all, the universal and ethical deity before whom all other gods or powers or idols must bow. The *Upanishads* take over the reincarnation myth somewhat as a twentieth century Christian theologian might take over one of the prevalent contemporary anthropologies such as, say, a Freudian or Marxist one, and, baptizing it, adapt it to Christian use. Christianity, indeed, not only underwent a similar process long ago when its first contact with the Gentile world forced its hellenization; it had been already pre-hellenized with the hellenization of Judaism before the Christian era.

The appeal of the reincarnation myth to the upanishadic mind is understandable. The *Upanishads* appeared at a stage when the learned were seeing the futility of mere cultic ritual. So one of the *Upanishads,* for instance, warns against relying on the ritual sacrifices to save one from rebirth.[8] These sacrifices are called "unsafe boats". No, the only way is the practice of austerity (*tapas*) and faith (*śraddhā*).[9] Salvation is to be found in the forest rather than the market-place. It is by knowledge; yet the knowledge is not of the informational kind. It is, rather, what in a tradition more directly affecting Western culture was called *gnosis*. That is, the knowledge is understood somewhat as a grasp of the fundamental chemistry of the spiritual world. It is not a knowledge that is imparted by the acquisition of facts. It is not poured into the mind as would be so many marbles into a bottle. A teacher or guru may assist him who would attain this esoteric knowledge; but at most such a teacher can be no more than what Socrates called himself: a mere midwife. The student himself must find his own way and he does so by rigorous discipline of his whole being. We may understand this kind of knowledge better if we call it wisdom, and self-discipline is the beginning of it.

Characteristically, the writers of the *Upanishads* do not all give the same account of the nature of the process of rebirth. What they do commonly tend to assume is that it is something undesirable. That assumption underlies the whole development of the *karma-saṁsāra* presupposition. It determined the form of reincarnation doctrine that was to become so basic to later Indian thought and that was to be exported so influentially by Buddhist missionaries to other Asiatic cultures, notably to China and Japan. Reincarnation, far from being an answer to a religious question, becomes the question demanding an answer. The answer is always soteriological: it tells you how you may hope to get out of the cycle of rebirth, the thought of which is assumed to be oppressive to every reflective person. Karma, far from being a religious tenet, has become, rather, a moral and metaphysical assumption about the nature of existence, in face of which religions are expected to provide a way out. The great religions that India has cradled, such as Vedanta, Jainism and Buddhism, have all, each in its own way, attempted to provide answers to the question. They do not argue for reincarnation as, say, a seventeenth century Jesuit might have argued against a Dominican for the Immaculate Conception of Mary. They assume it as a modern existentialist psychologist assumes that his patient is in a state of *Angst* and is looking for a way out. If he expounds the notion of *Angst* to his patient it is only by way of defining the problem more clearly to the patient's mind. In short, in the oriental religions, reincarnation is not a religious tenet; it is, rather, a presupposition that poses typically religious questions. When an occidental who has become attracted to oriental religion hears of the doctrine of reincarnation, he may well ask excitedly: "Is it really true that I may hope to come back to earth again?" No one born into a Hindu or Buddhist society would put the question that way. In such cultures, when a religious inquirer asks anything such as what the rich man in the Gospels asked Jesus ("Good Master, what shall I do that I may inherit eternal life?"),[10] he is more probably expecting to be told how to break the chain of rebirth and escape to what lies beyond it.

The myth of reincarnation may be interpreted, then, in many different ways. Pythagoras, on the one hand, if we are to believe his biographer Diogenes Laertius, seems to have taken human rebirth literally, for (according to Diogenes) Pythagoras was accustomed to say he had formerly been Aethalides, then Euphorbus, and that he had been mortally wounded by Menelaus at the siege of Troy.[11] Plato, on the other hand, as is well-known, used transmigration as part of the general mythological scenery available in his time; but how precisely he regarded it is unclear. We know only that he made use of the notion in presenting his own thought, as he made use of other popular myths of his day.

The myth of reincarnation has also, however, an obvious connection with what Professor Eliade has called the myth of the eternal return, which represents the rhythm of birth, death and rebirth as a cyclic reality at the core of the whole universe. "According to this doctrine," he writes, "the universe is eternal but it is periodically destroyed and reconstituted every Great Year." This "Great Year" seems to be a Chaldean notion which, in a popularized form, spread through the Hellenic world in the third century before the Christian era, dominating, for example, the thought of Zeno and the Stoics. "The myth of universal combustion was decidedly in fashion throughout the Roman-Oriental world from the first century B.C. to the third century of our era; it successively found a place in a considerable number of gnostic systems derived from Greco-Irano-Judaic syncretism." Such ideas, which are to be found among the Mayas and the Aztecs as well as in India and Iran recognize cyclical catastrophe as a normal incidence in the periodicity of the universe.[12] In Hindu mythology the present aeon began as in a beautiful springtime of joy; but it disintegrates, till at last it is destroyed by Shiva's dancing feet. Then comes about the rebirth of the world, sustained by the laughing Vishnu, and so on in an endless cycle. This notion of a cyclic universe appears in innumerable forms in the history of religion. The wheel of rebirth is well-known in Buddhist art. In ancient Greece we find it in Orphism. It is also represented in the legend of the phoenix, a mythical bird supposed to live for many centuries, which cremates itself on a funeral pile and rises youthfully from its own ashes to live through another cycle. The phoenix legend appears in various forms in regions as remote from one another as Egypt and Ireland, Turkey and Japan. The phoenix even appears also in some rabbinical lore.

Since a cyclic view of the universe and the reincarnationist implications of such a view were part of the general stock in trade of the Gnostic systems that were so influential in the intellectual climate of the Mediterranean world in New Testament times, when Christianity was spreading to the Gentile world, such notions inevitably entered to some extent into the thought and language of those who taught the Christian Way. Within about a century of the death of Christ, Justin Martyr, after much searching among the viable alternatives of his time (and there were many), embraced the Christian Way. According to the *Dialogue with Trypho,* he taught that human souls inhabit more than one body in the course of their earthly pilgrimage.[13] He even suggested the possibility that those who live such carnal lives that they deprive themselves of the capacity to see God may be reincarnated as beasts. Christians who taught the pre-existence of the soul came to be known as the *pre-existiani.* As we shall see in a later chapter, Origen certainly taught a doctrine of pre-existence of the soul and probably taught a form of reincarnationism, and his influence, as the greatest thinker of his day in the Christian Church, was immense. Several circumstances, however, conspired to inhibit official acceptance of reincarnationism.

Probably the most powerful among these was the extremely apocalyptic character of the primitive Christian temper. In the first century, the *parousia* or Second Coming of Christ was expected imminently, and with it the rolling up of the present world "like a scroll." Then would come a new and better order under Christ's kingship. In such a climate of expectancy Christians could have little interest in speculations about the pre-existence of the soul, and less still in reincarnationism. Indeed, when people feel the end of the world is at hand they have no interest in any kind of philosophical speculations. They are filled, rather, with a sense of the urgency of the situation and of the need for repentance and preparation. When you think you may have only a few months left to live, or even a few years, you are unlikely to be well disposed toward wrestling with a speculative metaphysical system. You are much more likely to be concerning yourself with the immediate, practical questions with which your sense of the approaching end confronts you. A man who sees himself engaged in a last, brief, ferocious duel with Satan, with the prize of paradise awaiting him at the end of his final ordeal, will treat metempsychosis as impatiently as a soldier in a bayonet charge would treat one of Spinoza's scholia. That is not to say, however, that he would necessarily be repudiating it; it is only to say he has no time for it.

Theoretically, as the eschatological hope of the Church gradually came to be reinterpreted as less imminent, interest in the themes of pre-existence and metempsychosis might be expected to reawaken. To some extent, indeed, as we have seen, that did occur. Other factors, however, emerged. Gnosticism was a prevailing mood, a fashionable *genre* of religious thought in the early centuries of the Christian era, rather than a specific cult or school. It was a syncretistic, eclectic amalgam of religious ideas. That was the climate in which Christianity emerged and developed in the Gentile world. The Church, institutionally and administratively, to say nothing of other considerations, could not extend unlimited hospitality to *all* such ideas. Recent scholarship and archeological discoveries show, indeed, that the extent to which Gnostic ideas affected early Christian thought was even greater than has been commonly recognized. Nevertheless, if all Gnostic ideas had been allowed free entry into the Church, Christianity would have become a mere clearing-house of religious ideas. As such it could not easily have survived in competition with influential schools such as Neoplatonism. For unlike Hinduism, which has flourished as such a clearing-house, Christianity had no racial cohesion. Hinduism, for all its hospitality to religious ideas, even to logically incompatible systems, is fundamentally and institutionally the religion of the Indus Valley. Like Judaism, it has opened its doors to all comers; but the fact that an Icelander can become a Hindu or a Jew if he chooses does not diminish the importance of the fact that both these religions have a deep foundation in blood and soil. Christianity, as it developed in the Gentile world, had none. The difference is enormous. Buddhism, when it left its Hindu parent stem and, in its Mahayana form, spread as a great international religion to China, Tibet and Japan, had no effective competitor outside India where it had been cradled. Meanwhile, in India it could not compete with its spiritual Mother, which characteristically reabsorbed its reforming ideas. Both the historical circumstances of Christianity and the problems it had to face were so thoroughly different as to be incomparable.

The point of these observations should not be difficult to see. The Church, in its discriminating attitude toward fashionable Gnostic doctrines, was in no mood to give its approval to any dogmas at all. It was in principle disinclined to make formulations, except to the extent that it was forced to do so by external pressure. When doctrines were formulated, their entailments had to be considered, of course; but the tendency of the Church, when acting institutionally, was to set aside whatever it was not forced to formulate, more especially if it had Gnostic overtones and seemed to lack clear biblical support. All the prevailing theories about pre-existence would seem to fall under this head.

We shall have to devote more attention to some of these ques-

tions and treat them in greater detail later. My purpose in mention-
ing them at this stage is, rather, to illustrate the nature of the
problem that lies before us. In the history of religion the myth of
reincarnation has generally been understood as an expression of
certain presuppositions about the human plight. It has functioned
somewhat as the prison motif functions in modern existentialist
literature. As the existentialist assumes that only the most obtuse
need to be told they are imprisoned by circumstance, so the reincarnationist has usually taken for granted that all but the most
purblind of sensuous men and women will see at once that we are,
at least *in one way or another,* caught in a cycle that determines our
destiny. He assumes that if there is to be controversy, it can only
be about the solution to the problem that all thoughtful people
already recognize. A typical solution in the more developed, ethical versions embraces acceptance of the notion that we are able
through the exercise of our free will to achieve release, to break the
chain.

What exactly the chain is and how it may be broken is soterio-
logically less important. Does it matter whether the bog you are
sinking in be quicksand or mud? Does it matter whether you are
pulled out of it by a rope or by a crane? In such a predicament will
you boggle at whether you land in forest, meadow or stream? So to
the man in the grip of the chain of rebirth and under the law of
karma, whether the proposed solution is to achieve resurrection or
nirvana, eternal rest or work-without-weariness, seems existen-
tially beside the point. He will say, rather: "Let me out first and I'll
talk theology afterwards." Similarly, it will seem to matter little
whether metempsychosis is taken literalistically or figuratively,
whether it is technically to be dubbed a doctrine of pre-existence or
called by some Sanskrit name. The authentic seeker is likely to be
minimally interested in the aetiology of his predicament and
maximally interested in the cure. In the New Testament language
he will ask, "What shall I do to be saved?" Only when he has
received a satisfactory answer (*tapas* or "sell all that thou hast" or
the like) will he be in a mood to speculate on either the nature of the
human predicament or the destiny of man.

But when all that is said, the prevalence of the myth of reincarnation, when it is not artificially inhibited in ways we have just seen
exemplified, is very remarkable indeed. Eliade has persuasively
argued that "the archaic evaluation of death as the supreme means
to spiritual regeneration founded an initiatory scenario which sur-

vives even in the great world religions and is re-valorised also in Christianity. . . . But . . . if one is continually dying countless deaths in order to be reborn to *something else* . . . then one is . . . growing more and more into immortality.''[14] What is especially remarkable is that the myth of reincarnation should have been in such persistent use as the vehicle man's expression of his deepest level of existential anguish. The myth of reincarnation has not only flourished in India and the Far East, where it has been thoroughly domesticated since long before the Christian era, but has persistently recurred over and over again even in the most inauspicious circumstances and in face of ideologically hostile environments.

Modern parapsychologists, psychic researchers, and other scientific investigators have made serious studies of claims to recollections of a previous life. The literature on the subject is considerable; the results, though they leave many unresolved puzzles, are inconclusive. The investigators, after disposing of numerous cases that are easily shown to be spurious, have unearthed some that cannot be treated so cavalierly. A noteworthy researcher in this special field is Ian Stevenson, M.D., Carlson Professor of Psychiatry, University of Virginia. When cases of children's claims to recollections of a previous life have been brought to him, his principal method has been first to cross-examine them on these alleged recollections, then to take the child to the environment in which he or she claims to have lived in the alleged previous life, and finally to have the child identify the supposed former relatives, neighbors and friends, whom he independently cross-examines.

Stevenson's methods also include the examination of birthmarks and deformities. For there is a common suggestion that a violent death, for instance by a bullet wound, may result in a birthmark in the next incarnation at the site of the wound inflicted in the previous life! One of his subjects, a Turk, claimed to have been, in his previous life, a gangster in Istanbul who was killed in a struggle with police. He pointed to a spot on his head where, he claimed,.the bullet had entered. Stevenson, after having made a notation of the facts as claimed, reflected that if the bullet had entered the Turk's head at that spot and in the direction that had been indicated in the claim, then it must have exited at another spot, the location of which could be approximately determined. He then went back to re-examine the Turk's head. The hair was bushy at the hypothetical spot, so that no birthmark could be easily detected. After Stevenson had parted the Turk's hair, however, he found exactly the sort of second birthmark he had hypothecated, though the Turk claimed at that time never to have known anything about such a mark. He has had also numerous other cases of children and other persons who, having been taken to the locale of an alleged previous existence, which they could not have visited before in their present life, recognized family members by name and knew a good deal about their history, sometimes even including information that may be presumed to have been unknown to anyone still alive at the time of the investigation.[15]

The myth of reincarnation presents us, then, with some remarkable puzzles, which even the most skeptical cannot well discard as entirely trivial. It is an ancient myth; yet it continues to flourish. Predominantly associated with the Orient, it has also, as we shall see, a long history in the West. The task that lies ahead of us must include an investigation into the meaning of the myth. How is it to be understood? In what way may it be adapted to the religious quests of today? What *kind* of answer does it call for in the light of modern knowledge and the contemporary situation? Before we consider such questions, however, we shall do well to look further into the historic role of the myth in those Western societies and cultures in which it is for one reason or another not patently indigenous.

REFERENCES AND NOTES

[1]O. Cullmann, *Immortality of the Soul or Resurrection from the Dead?* (New York: Macmillan Co., 1958); J. Pelikan, *The Shape of Death* (Nashville, Tenn.: Abingdon Press, 1961); H. Thielicke, *Death and Life* (Philadelphia: Fortress Press, 1970); original German edition: *Tod und Leben* (Tubingen: J.C.B. Mohr, 1946).

[2]Pelikan, *Shape of Death,* pp. 5, 121.

[3]J. Baillie, *And the Life Everlasting* (New York: Oxford University Press, 1966), p. 198.

[4]Thielicke, *Death and Life,* p. 196.

[5]Ibid., p. 197.

[6]See *Atharva-Veda:*12. 2, 52b. Cf. *Rig-Veda:* I, 164, 30 and 38.

[7]*Chāndogya Upanishad:*5, 3,:6, 1, 2.

[8]*Muṇḍaka Upanishad:*1, 2, 7.

[9]Ibid:1, 2, 11.

[10]Mark:10.17.

[11]Diogenes Laertius, *The Lives and Opinions of Eminent Philosophers,* Book 8, Chapter 4.

[12]Mircea Eliade, *The Myth of the Eternal Return* (New York: Pantheon, 1954), p. 87.

[13]*Dial.* IV (*P.G.* 6, cols. 481-484).

[14]Mircea Eliade, *Myths, Dreams and Mysteries* (New York: Harper Torchbooks, 1960; original French edition 1957), p. 227.

[15]*See* Bibliography.

IV

REINCARNATION IN JEWISH, ISLAMIC AND CHRISTIAN THOUGHT

> *As he went on his way Jesus saw a man blind from his birth. His disciples put the question, "Rabbi, who sinned, this man or his parents? Why was he born blind?"*
>
> John 9. 1-3

Reincarnation was certainly not part of the principal ideological furniture of the Bible as it was of the literature of India that was the heritage of the Buddha. Nevertheless, it was not entirely alien to the late Hebrew thought that was current at the time of Christ, which was already extensively affected by notions from the Hellenic world. It is possible that the Tanaiim, who were to be found in Jerusalem as early as the third century B.C. and were later acclaimed as the spiritual ancestors of the medieval kabbalists, may have taught reincarnationist views. Such views seem to have been congenial to Jewish teachers nearer the time of Jesus. Hillel and the Alexandrian Philo Judaeus may have been among these.

The Lord's word to Jeremiah is: "Before I formed thee in the belly I knew thee; and before thou camest forth out of the womb I sanctified thee, and I ordained thee a prophet unto the nations."[1] By the time of Christ the notion that the human soul is immortal had become part of the teaching of various Jewish groups and sects. The Pharisees, for instance, were among those who sub-scribed to that doctrine. Josephus, the Jewish historian, reports that they held that the souls of all men are incorruptible, and that while the souls of the wicked are to be consigned to eternal punishment, those of good men are removed into other bodies.[2] The Essenes, he tells us, held that while the human body is corrupt-ible the soul is immortal. It comes out of "the most subtile air." By a sort of natural magnetism it is enticed into the prison of the body, but at death it is released and mounts joyfully upward.

In the kabbalistic tradition, claiming hidden or secret wisdom, reincarnation is a central notion. Rabbi Chajim Vital, expounding the teaching of Rabbi Isaac Luria, the sixteenth century founder of a kabbalistic school in Spain, wrote a work called *Otz Chüm (The Tree of Life)* which expresses typically reincarnationist teachings. Yalkut Reubeni, reflecting an attitude that sounds very chauvin-istic today, warned that a man who is stingy with his talents and possessions shall be punished by being reincarnated as a woman! Reincarnationist notions are so deeply written into that esoteric Jewish literature that those Jews who follow the kabbalistic way make reincarnation sound almost an essential of the Jewish faith.

Not disconnected with kabbalism is the mystical movement called Hasidism, which has been very influential in Jewish life. In Hasidism reincarnation became a universally accepted belief, familiar in Yiddish literature, being clearly taught in recent times in, for instance, the *Dybbuk,* a popular mystical legend by S. Ansky (Solomon Judah Lob Rapoport) and in the writings of Sholem Asch.

Since Judaism is capable of such a striking development of reincarnational doctrine, the suggestions of it that we find in the New Testament need come as no surprise. According to John the Evangelist, when the disciples saw a man blind from birth, they wondered aloud who had sinned, he or his parents.[3] If it had been he, then he must have sinned in a previous life. The question appears to be, then: "How is the presence of an innate affliction like this to be squared with the justice of God? By the inheritance of the results of sin or by reincarnationist doctrine?" According to Matthew, the disciples, when Jesus asked whom people took him to be, ventured various possibilities they had heard, for instance, Elijah or Jeremiah.[4]

Reincarnationist views were commonplace in the Gnostic climate in which Christianity developed. Gnosticism, an amalgam of presuppositions that permeated the Mediterranean lands, is known to have been influential in primitive Christianity, and recent textual discoveries are showing more than ever how influential it was. Though Gnostic tendencies came under suspicion and eventually under the condemnation of the Church, Gnostic teachings were a live option for the earliest generation of Christians.[5] To belong to the group called the *pre-existiani,* who taught a transmigrationist type of doctrine, was by no means looked upon with the disfavor that adherence to such views eventually evoked. Clement of Alexandria, though his teaching is not unambiguous, was certainly interested, to say the least, in speculation about what he called *metensomatosis.*[6] The fact that Tertullian, one of the earliest of the Latin Fathers of the Christian Church, writes as vehemently as he does against reincarnationist interpretations of Christian belief is eloquent witness to the widespread influence of such views that, according to him, merited such denunciation.

The case of Origen merits special notice. Not only is his name associated with reincarnation, rightly or wrongly; he was beyond doubt the greatest biblical scholar as well as the most original philosophical mind of his age. Born about 185, he died about 254. His aim was to produce a systematic Christian philosophy, firmly based on the Bible. For one reason or another, he came to be associated with views that were accounted heretical. The political circumstances attending his condemnation and the theological consequences of his teaching are both such complex questions that a separate chapter will be devoted to him and his school. As we shall see in that next chapter, reincarnationist views, being associated with Origen, fell into disrepute because people erroneously supposed that a general council of the Church had condemned him and therefore his doctrine of the pre-existence of the soul.

The Council of Lyons in the thirteenth century and the Council of Florence in the fourteenth seem to presuppose that reincarnation had been anathematized, and they insisted that at death souls go immediately to heaven, hell or purgatory. We have seen, however, and we shall see more fully later, that a doctrine of purgatory such as was developed in the Middle Ages is compatible with a form of reincarnationist theory. Orthodox theological opinion during the Middle Ages nevertheless certainly discountenanced reincarnationist doctrine. Despite its repudiation by the custodians of Christian orthodoxy (what was taken to be the deposit of faith delivered to the apostles), it persistently appeared over and over again in innumerable sects, notably the Albigenses (Cathari) in the West, who were especially influential in southern France, the Paulicians and Bogomils in the East, and various esoteric societies, heretical groups, and underground movements all over Europe. The Albigenses, who, because of their uncompromising spirit-matter dualism, have been called the medieval Manichees, were conspicuously neo-Gnostic in their general outlook. They were clearly reincarnationist, teaching that the reason for our being on this earth at all is that we are fallen spirits forced to be incarcerated in bodies and to work out our liberation through transmigration from one body to another. Their teaching on reincarnation closely resembled forms of karmic doctrine in India; but they saw in Christ the instrument of divine redemption from the wheel of rebirth.

The seventh century of the Christian era saw the rise of Islam. Muhammad had sought acceptance from Jews and from Christians and had been ill received by both. The establishment of Islam is perhaps the most astonishing story of rapid missionary success in the history of religion. Islam spread quickly throughout the Arab lands. Before long it extended from Persia to Spain; eventually it spread to that region of the Indian sub-continent we now call Pakistan, and even to the Far East. The Islamic Empire, however enlarged by *jihad* (holy war), was sustained by a popular faith in the unity and sovereignty of Allah, a faith intentionally monolithic in its simplicity. It could be summed up in a few words that the muezzin still proclaims from the minaret of the mosque. *La ilāha illa Allāh; Muhammad rasūl Allāh:* there is no God but Allah, and Muhammad is his prophet. The popularity of the Muslim faith and practice owes much to that startling simplicity. Anyone, however unlettered, can quickly grasp the fundamentals of Islam, finding peace in its ethical ideals and satisfaction in the uncomplicated principles of its faith.

Yet the very simplicity of that faith as understood by the masses left open vast areas of philosophical speculation. From early in the history of Islam a tension developed between what today we should call religion and science: the revelation of the Qur'ān on the one hand and, on the other, philosophical inquiry and those scientific researches for which, in the Middle Ages, the Arab world was famed. Within that larger frame of reference, ideas alien to the simplicity, not to say naivety, of popular Muslim teaching, could move freely. The Arab philosophers were especially dependent upon Greek sources. No less than St. Augustine, and through him the whole of Western Christendom, the Arab thinkers were deeply indebted to the Neo-Platonic tradition. With such an intellectual heritage, and in the peculiar kind of freedom the Arab thinkers devised for themselves within Islam, transmigrationist notions inevitably appeared within a culture that at first sight might seem to be inhospitable to them. While the unlettered unquestioningly accepted the basic principles they were taught and the thoughtless among the better educated read the Qur'ān with uncompromising literalism, others held, not implausibly, that it had an internal as well as an external meaning. With such an esoteric interpretation, reincarnational views found a foothold.

In the teaching of the Sufis, who claimed to know the esoteric teaching behind the Qur'ān, reincarnation had a prominent place. Some of the great Sufi teachers got into trouble on account of their special claims. In the tenth century, Mansur Al-hallāj, for instance, claimed to be one with God, which of course was treated as the height of blasphemy. He was executed; but others of the Sufi Way exercised great influence in Islam. Through them and other channels, reincarnationist ideas passed into Islamic literature. The Druses, one of the most interesting groups in the Middle East today, have an obscure history, and they are notoriously disinclined to discuss their religious practices in detail; but reincarnation is indubitably both basic to and prominent in their beliefs. Being responsible members of society, they generally command the respect of their neighbors. The group who received me in northern Israel some years ago were singularly attractive people, cleanly, courteous and hospitable. The women, dressed in modest dark blue dresses, struck me as especially fine representatives of the best in the culture of the Middle East.

Judaism, Christianity, and Islam belong to a group of institutional religions whose ideas are culturally rooted in Semitic life and patterns of thought. Yet even in this relatively unpromising soil, reincarnational understandings of human destiny found an unexpected home, patristic controversies, conciliar anathemas, and medieval persecutions notwithstanding. In the post-medieval world right down to the present day, wherever ideas have flowed freely, its influence, among those who have any interest at all in questions about afterlife and human destiny, and who find no particular reason to repudiate reincarnation on dogmatic grounds, has continued to be astonishingly persistent. We must look at that spectrum of influence, however cursorily, if only to take the measure of what reincarnationist views may mean for our own culture and what their acceptance might portend for the future of Christian thought and life. First, however, let us consider, as promised, the early Christian controversy that had its focus in the work of Origen, who was by far the most remarkable genius, with the possible exception of Augustine, among the Christian Fathers, whose writings have commanded a greater authority in the Church than any other literature other than the Bible itself.

REFERENCES AND NOTES

[1]Jeremiah 1:4-5. On sources for the doctrine of reincarnation in Judaism, see A. Orbe, "Textos y pasajes de la Escritura interesados en la teoria de la reincorporación" in *Estudies Ecclesiasticos* (1959), pp. 77-91.

[2]Flavius Josephus, *The Jewish War*. Translated by W. Whiston, II, 8, 14.

[3]John 9, 1-3.

[4]Matthew 16, 13-14.

[5]For recent studies of Gnostic influence, see Geo Widengren, *Proceedings of the International Colloquium on Gnosticism* (held in Stockholm, August 1973). Leiden: E. J. Brill, 1977.

[6]See *Stromata* 4.26, for example. Not all would take such passages in Clement as decisive. Nevertheless, Photius, in the ninth century, charges Clement with having taught reincarnationist doctrine. (Libr. 109.)

V

THE ATTACK ON ORIGEN

> . . . *we have existed from the beginning,*
> *for in the beginning was the Logos. . . .*
> *Not for the first time does* [*the Logos*] *show*
> *pity on us in our wanderings; he pitied us*
> *from the beginning.*
>
> Clement of Alexandria, *Stromata*

The story of Origenism is peculiarly relevant to our study. Traditionally, Origen, the most learned as well as the most original thinker among the early Christian Fathers, has been accounted heterodox. Since his name has been associated with reincarnationist ideas, and since he has been generally supposed to have deviated from orthodox teaching, people have usually assumed that reincarnationism, however interesting or attractive, is completely out of the question as a Christian option.

The historical facts are far from supporting any such cut and dry view of the matter. The facts are, indeed, exceedingly complicated. Disentangling them is a laborious, not to say tedious, process; yet such is Origen's importance for our theme that we must inspect closely the circumstances that led to the ill repute of this enormously impressive Christian scholar. The outcome of the story is not conclusive; but such facts as we do know will enable a reader who is patient enough to attend to them to make up his own mind about their significance. In any case, the story, even apart from its indispensability for our investigation, is a fascinating epic.

For it shows how the Church has somehow survived even the most resolute attempts to destroy her by that formidable combination of stupidity and turpitude, political and ecclesiastical, that finds expression in a seemingly dedicated enmity to the use of the human mind in questions about religion.

The basic facts of Origen's life that have come down to us from antiquity are recorded by Eusebius (*c.* 260 - *c.* 340 A.D.), Bishop of Caesarea and commonly accounted "the Father of Church History." Origen, as we have already briefly noted, was born about the year 185 A.D., in Egypt, probably at Alexandria. At home he received a thoroughly Christian education. He is generally believed to have studied later under Clement of Alexandria, though some scholars have questioned this.[1] During the persecution of Christians in 202 A.D., Origen's father was killed, and we have a hint of the intensity of the young man's temperament in the recorded story that he was so bent on following his father by going out to invite martyrdom for himself that his mother had to hide his clothes to impede him from carrying out his rash enterprise. When Clement fled the persecution, he was succeeded by Origen as head of the catechetical school of Alexandria. That Origen should have been able to assume such intellectual leadership at so early an age attests the precocity of his genius. Hardly less remarkable was his self-discipline. The much recounted story of the excess of zeal that caused him to emasculate himself, taking literally the injunction of the Gospel,[2] has brought him considerable notoriety. It must be understood in the context of the age in which he lived and the circumstances of his life. At any rate, despite his youthful impetuosities, he matured to lead an immensely productive and influential life of scholarship and teaching. Finally, he was imprisoned in the persecution under Decius in 250 A.D., was severely tortured, and died a few years later.

As is to be expected in such an intellectual giant, he was a controversial figure in his own time and has long remained so. On the one hand he gained wide popularity; on the other, he met with intense hostility. The leaders of the Church have seldom been kind to its thinkers. Because of later condemnation of his teachings, though also no doubt partly on account of the inordinate length of his writings, most of the original Greek text of his works have been lost and survives only in fragments or in Latin translation. For this reason we are unable to know for certain what precisely were his opinions on all the subjects on which views have been attributed to him. Nevertheless, the general direction of his thought is clear.

Origen indubitably sought to ground all his teaching in Holy Scripture; but he was profoundly influenced by the Platonism that permeated the intellectual climate of Alexandria. He may properly be called a Christian Platonist. Indeed, it would have been impossible for anyone nurtured as he was in that climate, and on the Greek classics, to have escaped that very pervasive influence. One of the typically Platonic doctrines that affected Origen's thought was that the soul, being independent of the body and superior to it, is at its best when free of its attachment to the body. Attachment to the body, therefore, comes to be regarded as an imprisonment. Nevertheless, the body, though an obstacle, is also an instrument. Such a doctrine of the soul is, of course, *conducive* to a reincarnationist view such as is found in Plato's own writings.

In Origen's most important work, the *De Principiis* (Περὶ Ἀρχῶν) has come down to us a systematic and philosophical exposition of Christian theology. Axiomatic is the view that God is One and transcends his creation. On this most fundamental point he is unquestionably orthodox, being completely inhospitable to all pantheistic systems. As already noted, he is also thoroughly biblical; nevertheless, in accordance with the Alexandrian temper, he is disposed to read the Bible allegorically. He recognized three senses in which Scripture may be understood, the literal, the moral, and the allegorical or figurative. When in doubt, he prefers the allegorical. This aspect of his methodology is important for us, since it means that he would be open to such doctrines as reincarnation if they seemed to be implicit in the text, or if the text even permitted such an interpretation, always provided, of course, that no objection could be seen on other grounds. Origen saw the whole cosmos as pervaded with symbols of a world beyond, an invisible world reminiscent of Plato's World of Forms. So he could see two ways of responding to divine revelation: (1) the simple faith of untrained minds that cannot get beyond this way of responding, and (2) the ascent of the mind to the contemplation of God. The intellectually gifted cannot be blamelessly content with literalism; they must engage, somewhat after the manner of Plato's philosopher-kings, in contemplation of the eternal verities. Origen imposes on the learned the duty of coping with a tension he sees between Christian thought and Christian life. As a Christian thinker he is inevitably a lonely figure: too speculative for simple hearts, too biblical for philosophers.

So creative is Origen that one of the difficulties in interpreting him is that one is not always sure whether he is proposing a doctrine or only suggesting it as an explorable possibility. In any case, lack of the original texts leaves us often wondering to what extent his work has been tampered with in attempts either to whitewash supposed heresies or to implicate him in holding opinions he may not in fact have maintained. Certain doctrines, however, seem to be attributable to him.

The creative act of God is eternal. God is, we might say, Creator *par métier:* if God ever ceased to create he would cease to be God. God creates spirits, and all spirits are created equal. All are endowed with free will, through the exercise of which they develop. Some, falling into sin, either become demons (evil spirits) or else become imprisoned in bodies. This process of growth and retardation is an ongoing one. A human being, on death, might develop into an angel or demon. All this entails, of course, a highly allegorical interpretation of Genesis. God, in his love, sends forth Christ to accomplish or to accelerate the redemptive process. In contrast to the earlier generations of Christians who had expected an imminent end to the present world, Origen envisioned a long evolution, extending over aeons. In the last resort, salvation would be universal, so that even the demons would be saved. Yet that is not to say that sin ever goes unpunished. "The soul that sins beyond a certain point can never again become what once it might have been. . . . The purified spirit will be brought home; it will no longer rebel; it will acquiesce in its lot; but it may never be admitted within that holy circle where the pure in heart see face to face."[3]

Origen certainly taught the pre-existence of the soul; but not only has the soul an existence before it acquires or is fettered to a human body; death, according to Origen, does not terminate its progress or exclude the possibility of regress.[4] He is plainly much interested in providing a plausible way of making sense of the soul's journey. Yet though one might expect Origen to embrace reincarnationism we do not find, in the extant text, any clear statement in support of it. On the contrary, he speaks of "the false doctrine of the transmigration of souls into bodies."[5] He seems to think that reincarnationism in the Pythagorean form that was transmitted to Plato implies a fatalistic conception of the soul's destiny and he rejects it apparently for that reason.[6] While he attacks the widespread notion of his day that the soul of a human being could ever be imprisoned in the body of a beast (which he considers unfitting for a creature made in the image of God),[7] he does concede that the notion of reincarnation is a very plausible one.[8] That fatalistic interpretation is not, of course, by any means essential to reincarnationist belief and would be rejected, for example, by modern theosophists and others for whom reincarnationism is a fundamental tenet.

One is left with the impression, over and over again, that Origen is attracted to reincarnationism but that some forms of it with which he is familiar are suspect in his mind. He considers at some length the alleged identity of John the Baptist with Elijah (John 1.21), whose return was expected (Malachi 3.23 f.), and here, after setting forth opinions on both sides, he emphasizes the difficulty of the question and the variety of problems it entails. He points out that not only should we have to inquire what happens to the soul when it departs this life; we should have to consider whether it is possible for it to enter a second body and, if so, whether the process takes the same time in every case and whether the arrangements are always the same. Further, we should have to inquire whether belief in such a reincarnationist process entails holding the eternality of the world.

These are, of course, all standard problems for any reincarnationist, and nobody could be interested in them who did not take reincarnationism very seriously. In the end, however, Origen, after judicially setting forth such possibilities and pointing out the difficulties inherent in them, concludes by reaffirming the complexity of the subject and stating that a solution of the difficulties would require the examination of a wide variety of scattered passages of Scripture. He proposes, therefore, to say no more on the subject, since it would require a separate treatment. He remarks, nevertheless, that the question the Jews asked John the Baptist presupposes "that they believed in metensomatosis, as a doctrine inherited from their ancestors and therefore in no way in conflict with the secret ἀπόρρητος teaching of their masters."

Cardinal Daniélou, in his notable work on Origen,[9] observes that the whole Origenistic system depends on two principles: the love of God and human freedom.[10] Later, he goes on to remark that certain texts in Origen seem to affirm that souls remain eternally free, and that the freedom they enjoy entails the possibility of further falls. In other words, one would expect from this consideration that souls can never attain a built-in security, for that would mean the loss of their freedom.[11] I would suggest, indeed, that such a state of affairs would seem to be implicit in *any* interpretation of Genesis, Origenistic or otherwise. How else could Lucifer have fallen in the first place, to say nothing of Adam and Eve? Are we to suppose that God created spirits who could fall, and then, through the Incarnation, so changed the cosmic arrangements as to ensure that falls, which have been occurring for so long, are to be in the long run ruled out?

Daniélou reminds us that the notion of the eternal possibility of falls is precisely the point at which Gregory of Nyssa thought Origen vulnerable, reproaching him with platonistic metempsychosis.[12] Daniélou thinks that Origen, through his doctrine of apocatastasis, overcomes this objection, but at the expense of one of the two fundamental principles of the Origenistic system, namely, human freedom. "The weak point in Origen's thought," writes Daniélou, "is, then, his doctrine of successive existences. Souls experience multiple incarnations and are not conscious, in the existence that follows, of the one that precedes. This is an echo of the Platonic doctrine of metempsychosis that has profoundly marked and warped this aspect of Origen's thought."[13] Gregory of Nyssa objected, not to the doctrine of apocatastasis, but to what he took to be Origen's deformation of it. He rejected Origen's notion of a return to "pure spirit", successive lives, and permanent instability.[14] Daniélou thinks Gregory "humbler" before the mystery of the apocatastasis, "seeing in it the supreme work of a love that does not violate freedoms. For him it means the certainty of the salvation that human nature irrevocably acquires in Christ, but that leaves to individual freedom the possibility of absconding from it."[15]

Recognition of the immensity of the power of God's love is, of course, fundamental to Christian faith. Assurance of salvation through Christ is the supreme joy of the Christian life. Yet if the love of God so completely demolishes human freedom, the question must always be: what does it mean to say I am saved at the cost of the destruction of my freedom? The whole splendor of the redemptive act of Christ lies in the fact that the self-emptying of God in Jesus Christ is held to be without injury to my freedom. I may appropriate or not the fruits of that redemption. Daniélou, in championing the now traditionalist resistance to the reincarnationist tendencies of Origen, cannot dare to acknowledge that Origen's greatness lies precisely there. So he can only, at this point, invoke "mystery".

What Origen held on the subject of reincarnation is obscure. His sympathy with transmigrationist ideas is obvious to all of us. Indeed, since the lack of any strong prejudice against reincarnation in the early stages of Christian thought made it, as we have seen in an earlier chapter, a possible option within the Church at that time, we cannot but expect him to take reincarnationism seriously. For anyone with his general inclinations and Alexandrian upbringing to have failed to do so would be odd, to say the least. Yet natural as it might seem for Origen to adopt reincarnationism in its classic, Pythagorean form, as the "other half", so to speak, of the pre-existence doctrine to which he certainly subscribed, he cannot easily do so. The reason is his rejection of Gnostic dualism and the cyclic theory of history in favor of what he takes to be the biblical view. On a thoroughly cyclic philosophy of history, a Christian would have to say that God will return to earth in Christ not once but an infinite number of times. Plainly, Origen cannot allow such a notion, and he thinks that because the consummation of the world is near, when "this present state of corruption will be changed into one of incorruption," the soul cannot come back several times into the conditions of the present life. Otherwise, on the cyclic view, there would be no end to such successive incarnations. What clinches the case against reincarnationism for Origen is precisely this: history is moving toward a goal, and the actions and experiences of the soul must therefore, he thinks, minister to that goal. He is able to defend his pre-existence theory by arguing partly from biblical texts and partly from the notion that the diversity within historical existence can be explained by the creative act of God. Reincarnationism did not seem to him to fit the Christian philosophy of history, despite what he felt was its rational appeal.

His adversaries, when they attacked his teaching about the future life, were less subtle and much less discriminating. Great importance was attached in the early centuries of the Church to the notion that, at the resurrection of the body, the dead would rise with the bodies they had had in life. Origen denied such an identity. He was accused of a large variety of heresies that included not only his pre-existence theory but also, for example, a form of trinitarian doctrine known as subordinationism. Moreover, as so often happens, disciples often traduced the master's teaching. Origenism was far more wayward than Origen ever could have been, with the result that his name came eventually to be associated with all sorts of strange opinions. He was charged, for instance, with teaching that at the resurrection bodies will assume a spherical form. Pre-existence was a prime target for attack and to undiscerning antagonists reincarnationism would seem included in the condemnation. Origenism soon became a handy basket into which to throw all opinions one disliked. The subtlety of Origen's thought was easily lost in such cheap ecclesiastical skirmishes.

Origenism became, in the late fourth century, the focus of an acrimonious controversy. Epiphanius opened the attack, which was taken up by Jerome who, having been an ardent defender of Origen, was persuaded, apparently as a result of conversation at Jerusalem with Epiphanius, to change sides and help to seek Origen's condemnation. The attempt boomeranged, for the bishop from whom Jerome sought Origen's condemnation not only did not provide it; he obtained from the secular authorities a sentence of exile against Jerome! Theophilus, Patriarch of Alexandria from the year 385 A.D., who seems to have been ambitious, not to say unscrupulous, in his efforts to advance the interests of his See, had been at one time a supporter of Origen and, like Jerome, had turned against him. He invoked a council at Alexandria which, in the year 400 A.D., condemned Origenism. Theophilus, continuing his campaign against Origen, called him the "hydra of heresies" and persecuted his adherents.

That there were political motives behind these moves may well be suspected. When the controversy was renewed in the sixth century, the political background is only too obvious and is well-known. Such were the circumstances attending the convocation of the Second Council of Constantinople (the Fifth Ecumenical Council of the Church) that some modern Roman Catholic scholars question whether the anathemas it issued bind the conscience of Roman Catholics today.

Before the council was convened, a bitter conflict had existed between the Emperor Justinian and Pope Vigilius. There can be no doubt that Vigilius was under much political pressure, and it seems clear that opponents of Origenism manipulated Justinian, turning his despotic tendencies to their political advantage. At any rate, the actions of Vigilius are difficult to follow: he vacillates; he reverses his own positions; yet he often shows great courage. Moreover, the name of Origen was almost certainly used by many as a cloak for promoting a pantheistic mysticism that was in vogue in some of the monastic centers in Palestine. Above all, the controversy over Origenism was embedded in a larger framework of controversy concerning other issues such as Monophysitism and

Nestorianism, so complicating matters further still. The dispute with which we are concerned here was only part, and probably not a conspicuously important part, of a very deep, impending schism between East and West which, though the breach did not become definite and formal till 1054, was already troubling the whole Christian Church.

Out of the labyrinth of political pressure, ecclesiastical intrigue, and theological acrimony, we cannot hope to nail down all the relevant facts; but some things do emerge from which at least tentative conclusions may be drawn. The anchorite-monks of the New Laura, near Jerusalem, who had separated from the monastery of the Great Laura, had been especially strong partisans of Origenism; but others also supported Origenist views. As I have already suggested in the preceding paragraph, the Origenist label was probably used to cover notions that were not at all taught by Origen, and that may have been indeed as remote from Origen's teaching as were those of the Neoplatonists from Plato's. Be that as it may, opponents of Origenism succeeded in getting the Emperor Justinian to write a letter to the Patriarch of Constantinople naming Origen as one of the pernicious heretics. At the command of Justinian, a synod was convened at Constantinople in 543 A.D., and an edict was issued, which set forth a list of errors attributed to Origen and purported to refute them. This edict, which was supposed to promote peace between East and West, divided them further. Pope Vigilius at first opposed the imperial edict and broke off communion with the Patriarch of Constantinople who supported it. Then when he arrived in Constantinople he reversed himself and, while being careful not to concede that the Emperor had any authority in theological matters, issued a document condemning writings that had been anathematized in the imperial edict. This document was much criticized by bishops in Gaul, North Africa, and elsewhere, and Vigilius withdrew it in 550 A.D..

The matters covered in these complicated moves were so extensive that it is virtually impossible to say what was really happening to the Origenist controversy in the course of the more comprehensive conflict within which it was considered. Meanwhile, the Origenist monks themselves became divided into two groups: the Isochrists and the Protoctists. The former held that eventually all human beings would become equal to Christ, while the latter denied this. The Isochrist notion is plainly in the direction of the kind of pantheism that we know to be so much associated with oriental forms of reincarnationist teaching and, we have seen from the outset of the present study, is quite incompatible with the Christian Way. The Protoctists, who opposed the Isochrists, ended, at any rate, by repudiating the doctrine of the pre-existence of the soul and joining forces with the opponents of Origenism.

After much discussion and many maneuvers, the Emperor Justinian called a council of the whole Church, known as the Second Council of Constantinople or Fifth Ecumenical Council of the Church, which met in 553 A.D.. The purpose was again to reconcile East and West, and therein it singularly failed. Justinian had hoped, by his edict, to conciliate the Monophysites (who held that Christ had only one nature, the divine) by displaying zeal in denouncing their opponents, the Nestorians. Monophysitism was a very widely held view within the Christian Church, and there are indeed several Churches today, such as the Coptic and the Ethiopic, that have remained avowedly Monophysite. Moreover, though Monophysitism was officially repudiated in the Catholic Church, popular medieval piety was immensely influenced by it. Justinian, in his edict of 543-544 A.D., had condemned writings sympathetic to Nestorius, in what came to be known as "The Three Chapters" (*ta tria kephalaia*). These writings had nothing to do with Origen at all, and it was principally on their account that the Fifth Ecumenical Council was held. The extent, if any, to which Origenism was really condemned at that ecumenical council is, to say the least, questionable. Justinian was in fact engaged in an attempt to attack the theological positions of the School of Antioch, which was opposed to that of the Alexandrian school of which Origen was the most brilliant representative. Not only was Justinian conspicuously unsuccessful in that enterprise; he succeeded in stirring up old controversies that might have died down but for his meddling.

The Ecumenical Council was convened on May 5, 553, under the presidency of the Patriarch of Constantinople; but the Emperor controlled the proceedings. The arrangements were stacked against the West. Of the 165 bishops who signed the acts of the Council at its final meeting on June 2, not more than six could have been from the West. In protest against that and other irregularities, Pope Vigilius refused to attend. So far as our present inquiry is concerned, the actual decrees of the Council are not clear. The Three Chapters were anathematized; but, as we have seen, they had nothing directly to do with Origen. Of the fourteen anathemas pronounced by the Council, Origen's name is mentioned in one, among a list of heretics; but there is some evidence that justifies a belief that this is an interpolation. Vigilius, in the long run, accepted the Council; but what precisely his acceptance means in terms of our subject is not at all clear. Even with his acceptance, however, the Council was not immediately recognized in the West as an ecumenical council of the Church. Some dioceses, including Milan, even broke off communion with Rome. Milan, indeed, remained out of communion with Rome till the end of the sixth century. It would be difficult to imagine a more inconclusive outcome, even if we could be sure, as we are not in respect of Origenism, what the inconclusiveness was about.

Origen, however, suffered even more from his friends than from his enemies. For when we come to ask, as we must, what precisely we know today of his views on reincarnation, we find we cannot really say what he held, because his friends imposed a sort of informal censorship on works and passages that seemed to them to besmirch his orthodoxy. So such works and passages that contained his more adventuresome and interesting ideas were allowed to disappear: disapproving scribes simply did not copy them. The only complete text of Origen's principal work, the *De Principiis,* that we now have is a free translation, the work of Tyrannius Rufinus (*c.* 345-410), the tendentious character of whose translations was pointed out by Jerome (*c.* 342-420), indisputably the greatest translator in the early Church. Rufinus bowdlerized Origen in the interests of protecting him from the charge of heresy. Evagrius Ponticus (346-99) developed a sort of super-Origenism that greatly aggravated the troubles that arose in the sixth century. Rufinus did the more harm, however, for while Evagrius helped to bring Origen into disrepute among the pious, Rufinus and the disapproving scribes have prevented us all, pious and impious alike, from knowing exactly what Origen held on reincarnation.

What, then, may we conclude on this tantalizing question? I am convinced that he taught reincarnationism *in some form*. No doubt here, as elsewhere, he chose to distinguish between ecclesiastical orthodoxy and his own views, as surely any original thinker inevitably would do. That would account for his being able to write, as we have seen he did, of "the false doctrine of the transmigration of souls into bodies."[15] Such a condemnation was no doubt somewhat like the Church of England's condemnation of "the Romish Doctrine concerning Purgatory,"[17] where that Church did not find itself in the least inhibited from developing, as we shall see later, an alternative interpretation of its own. As it denounced only "the Romish Doctrine concerning Purgatory," not the notion of purgatory itself, so the fact that Origen could write of "the false doctrine of the transmigration of souls into bodies" would not preclude his teaching an alternative one of his own.

The key may be found in his theory of aeons. According to this theory, the gradual progression toward the final restoration of all things takes an enormously long time, an incalculably long series of world ages or aeons. Origen seems free to propound a doctrine very like the Indian karmic one[18] together with a doctrine of Providence, while denying that he is really teaching reincarnation. For, according to Origen, each soul is embodied only once in each aeon, and he understands reincarnationism to mean multiple embodiments within a single age.[19] So we may well surmise that alongside the seemingly anti-reincarnationist passages that have survived the informal censorship of his friends, there were, in the original Greek text, others that today would be generally classified as no less clearly reincarnationist than are the *Upanishads* and the *Bhagavad Gita*.[20] His reincarnationist teachings, one may reasonably suspect, were lost in the ecclesiastical skirmishes, in the course of which Origenism became a handy basket into which to throw all opinions one disliked. No one accustomed to the stupid partisanship of ecclesiastical quarrels would find this view in the least implausible.

What is certain and may be tragic is that Christians have since generally believed (for not everyone can be expected to know of the muddle, obscurity and inconclusiveness of the politico-ecclesiastical proceedings) that reincarnation is incompatible with Christian faith. They have taken for granted, therefore, that it is a forbidden notion, to embrace that which is to renounce Christ and to abandon the Church, which is his Body. They have supposed, from what they have either read or heard from bishops, priests, and others on whom they have been accustomed to depend, that the Fifth Ecumenical Council had closed the door for ever. As already noted in an earlier chapter, both the Council of Lyons in 1274 and the Council of Florence in 1439 simply assume that reincarnationism (which by that time had appeared as a prominent tenet of the indubitably heretical Albigenses) had been long ago outlawed.

These medieval councils stressed the swift movement of the

soul, at the moment of death, to its final destiny: heaven or hell.
That proved, of course, a telling and sometimes fearsome point in
popular preaching. Yet the whole question of the soul's destiny
was and remained in such a chaotic state that one wonders how
even the less thoughtful among Christians could have been content
so to let it stay. The soul, separated from the body, goes straight to
heaven or hell. That is traditionally called the "particular" judgment. Yet at the "general" judgment souls are to have their bodies
returned to them (the very bodies they had inhabited on earth),
though what the bodies were to do for the souls that had apparently
functioned well enough without them, enjoying already the bliss of
heaven or suffering the torments of hell, must have been tantaliz-
ingly obscure to anyone who thought at all.

The difficulty of accounting for the temporarily discarnate soul
was aggravated by the ready acceptance by later medieval thinkers
of Aristotle's teaching. Aristotle, recovered in the twelfth century,
was to the great medieval thinkers the highest authority from the
side of what we today would call "the sciences" or "science". It
happened that his doctrine of the unity of body and soul seemed to
corroborate biblical teaching, for the earlier Hebrew conception
was that body and soul are one, being together the creation of God.
So the Platonic type of doctrine did not fit. Contrary, however, to
what is often supposed, Platonic and Neoplatonic notions deeply
influenced medieval thinkers even after Aristotle had been recovered. Aristotle challenged their minds, but Plato was nearer
their hearts. The common people, moreover, who did not care
much what Aristotle said, were instinctively ambivalent on such
matters: imbued with the notion that religion is a turning of the soul
inwards (and therefore away from the body), they were also (like
the biblical writers themselves) very earthy; hence the splendor of
Dante's literary achievement, which combines both aspects of the
medieval mind. At any rate, the apostolic emphasis on the resurrection of the body, contradistinguished from the old pagan notions of the immortality of the soul, was believed to be supported
by the "science" of the day, yet did not fit what theologians
commonly said about what happens at death. Pope Benedict XII,
for example, in his bull *Benedictus Deus,* issued in 1336, upheld
the doctrine that souls go at once either to heaven, hell or purgatory, so excluding the notion of "falling asleep" for a time, such as
had been characteristic of the thought of some of the early Christian Fathers.

The mention of purgatory calls to our attention, moreover, the fact that few people in the Middle Ages were bold enough to expect to go straight to heaven. Most would not feel holy enough for that. The ordinary expectation would be that, if saved at all, they would move at once to purgatory, spending some "time" there before going on to heavenly bliss. Purgatorial "time" was never definable. It was assumed, however (at any rate by the learned) to be different from earthly time. But then neither could the nature of purgatorial "fire" be intelligibly specified, though purgatory was always associated with purging by fire. In the absence of a body, it obviously could not be the kind of fire a chemist or physicist could examine.

The difficulties do not stop even there, for yet another state was envisioned: limbo. Traditionally, there are at least two kinds of limbo: the *limbus patrum* and the *limbus infantium*.[21] To the *limbus patrum* were assigned holy men and women who, having died before the time of Christ, had to await his descent to their abode to retrieve them and carry them up to heaven. That event was commonly supposed to have occurred between the death of Christ on Good Friday and his resurrection on Easter Day. It was a theme much depicted in medieval art, usually called the Descent into Hell or (in England) the Harrowing of Hell. The *limbus infantium* is the state of infants who die before baptism and are therefore (such was a widespread belief among medieval Christians) ineligible for heaven. Both forms of limbo were understood to be pleasant places or states, though not to be compared with the supernatural joy of heavenly bliss. The learned knew that limbo is to be understood as a state rather than a place (as are also to be understood the other possible destinations of humankind); but the problem of the functioning of the discarnate soul remained. It presented difficulties in terms of later medieval thought that must have been just as puzzling, in their way, as is the mind-body problem to contemporary philosophers. As we shall consider in a separate chapter, both modern philosophy and modern scientific thought are inhospitable to the notion of a discarnate soul.

REFERENCES AND NOTES

[1]*See,* for example, J. Munck, *Untersuchen über Klemens von Alexandria (Forschungen zur Kirchen und Geistesgeschichte* 2; Stuttgart, 1933), pp. 224-229.

[2]Matthew 19,12.

[3]Charles Bigg, *The Christian Platonists of Alexandria* (New York: AMS Press, Inc. 1970; first published 1886), p. 292.

[4]Thomas Aquinas observes *(Quaest. disp. de pot.,* q. 3, a.10), with his characteristic perspicacity, that all who have affirmed the existence of the soul before birth in a body admit, at least implicitly, a transmigrationist principle.

[5]*Commentary on Matthew* XIV, 10.20.

[6]*Contra Celsum,* 5.29.

[7]Ibid., 4.83.

[8]*Commentary on John* VI, 13.74.

[9]Jean Daniélou, *Origène.* (Paris: La Table Ronde, 1948).

[10]He cites: *De Principiis,* I, 8, 3 and III, 5, 6.

[11]Daniélou, p. 280.

[12]Here Daniélou cites, as texts that seem to confirm Gregory's charge: *Commentary on Matthew,* XIII, 12; *De Principiis,* III, 1, 23.

[13]Daniélou, p. 282.

[14]Daniélou cites Gregory: Migne, *Patres Graeci,* LXXXVI, 898 B and XLVI, 108 C, 109 C.

[15]Daniélou, p. 283.

[16]*Commentary on Matthew* XIV, 10.20.

[17]*Book of Common Prayer,* "Articles of Religion", Article XXII.

[18]*De Principiis,* I, 8; III, 1, 21 f., III, 3, 5.

[19]For Origen's theory of aeons, see *De Oratione,* XXVII, 14; *Commentary on Matthew,* XI, 3; XII, 36; XIV, 3.

[20]*See* the passage in *De Principiis,* IV, 4, 8, as preserved in Jerome and cited by him *(Ep. ad Avitum,* 14) as evidence that Origen taught the transmigration of souls.

[21]Cf. St. Thomas Aquinas, *3 Sent.,* distinctio 22, q. 2, a.1; *4 Sent.,* distinctio 45, q. 1, a. 2.

VI

REINCARNATION IN RENAISSANCE AND LATER LITERATURE

I am personally convinced beyond any shadow of doubt that reincarnation is a fact.

Lord Dowding, *Lynchgate*

That reincarnationist ideas should have continued to exert some underground influence in the Middle Ages is not particularly remarkable if, bearing in mind the intellectual chaos we have just considered, one remembers how pervasive had been the influence of Gnostic ideas in the Mediterranean cradle of the great religions of the West. Before the printing revolution in the fifteenth century, ideas travelled slowly. When you heard an idea that was new to you and that seemed to be condemned by those whom you accounted authoritative in such matters, either you rejected it out of hand on that account or else you took it underground, which has always been the safest place for incubating the most interesting ideas.

More interesting is the persistence of the theme in Renaissance literature and right down to modern times. The reincarnationist motif recurs over and over again, springing up in the most unexpected places. Many, among both naturalistic thinkers and others, have applauded the assertion *natura nihil agit frustra,* "nature does nothing in vain," which the seventeenth century physician, Sir Thomas Browne, in his famous *Religio Medici,* goes so far as to call "the only indisputable axiom in philosophy."[1] That celebrated author, while he did not subscribe to reincarnationist doctrine in any of the traditional forms in which it is found in India and elsewhere, accepted the old notion that there is "a piece of Divinity in us, something that was before the Elements," and he believed in a vague form of transmigrationism. Such a belief, imprecise or otherwise, seems to have been almost universal in humanistic thinkers in the aftermath of the sixteenth century Renaissance. The revival of Neo-Platonism at Florence, under Medici protection, set a widespread fashion in thought that naturally favored reincarnationist ideas such as were commonly associated with the Platonic tradition.

Reincarnationist notions found ready acceptance among the *umanisti,* the Italian humanists who especially flourished in the Quattrocento. Pico della Mirandola, a typical Italian Renaissance humanist, interested himself in kabbalistic and hermetic literature, teaching that at death the soul passes out of one body and enters another. The Neapolitan Giordano Bruno who had entered the Dominican Order as a boy of fifteen, became interested in hermetic literature and, besides upholding the Copernican cosmology, taught specific reincarnationist doctrines, being eventually burned at the stake in Rome on February 17, 1600. He was very influential after his death, not least on great seventeenth century rationalist philosophers such as Leibniz and Spinoza. In his profession of faith before the Inquisition he declared that though, speaking as a Catholic, he must say that the soul on death goes to heaven or hell or purgatory, yet as a philosopher who had given much thought to the question, he found reasonable the belief that, since the soul is other than the body and is never found apart from the body, it passes from one body to another, as Pythagoras long ago had taught.

These Italian Renaissance humanists were often deeply religious. Their opinions had almost nothing to do with what we today commonly understand as humanism. The term "humanism" is not found in English before the early nineteenth century, being an invention of Samuel Taylor Coleridge, who liked neologisms and adopted it to designate a theological position, namely that of one who denies the divinity of Christ. The term "humanist", however, had been in use centuries earlier, being found in Francis Bacon, for instance, who uses it in the old sense of the Italian "umanista", which had no such dogmatic overtones and no such negativity. It expressed, rather, a positive affirmation of the splendor of being human, and called on men and women to celebrate the sentiment of the famous line of Terence, *homo sum: humani nil a me alienum puto:* I am a human being; nothing human is alien to me. Far from being in any way anti-religious or an alternative to religion, it designated a literary person who, inheriting the openness of the Socratic tradition, welcomed religious ideas as inseparable from the fulfilment of human destiny. Some were even buried in the habit of a religious Order, as members of a secular group professing adherence to its ideals and following in some measure its rule. Marsiglio Ficino, writing to Lorenzo de' Medici, even claimed the title *sacerdos musarum* (priest of the Muses), accounting himself a priest of an artistic brotherhood within the Church rather than a rebel against it. Nor were the sources of the humanists' inspiration exclusively Graeco-Roman, as is often supposed. Such was their concern for the universality of man that they sought inspiration wherever it might be found. Oriental carpets are a feature of many Quattrocento pictures. Siennese painting, not least that of Francesco di Giorgio, reflects Indo-Persian motifs. The Gothic north no less than the Byzantine east served the purposes of those who had caught the spirit of the Renaissance. Such was the spirit of the age in which reincarnationist ideas prospered in a new way. For although the *umanisti* were, in the heyday of the new age, deeply reverent toward religious ideas, they had no interest in the traditional dogmatic theology of the Schools. They were open, therefore, to religious ideas of any kind that they thought they could fit into a Christian humanism. Nor was this attitude, in typical cases, merely eclectic. These humanists were far too deeply rooted in their Catholic heritage, and their minds were too accustomed to its conceptual archetypes, to allow them to indulge in any easygoing sort of eclecticism. When, therefore, we find them fascinated by reincarnationist themes, as we do, we may be sure that reincarnation is not, for them, but one among many capricious notions. It is a direction whither they naturally move as soon as they are loosed from the intellectual straightjackets of their heritage.

John Milton (1608-74) is by common consent one of the greatest poets in the literature of the world. Though as a Puritan his main appeal in theological matters was to the Bible, he was very learned in Christian literature and in many ways taught views that could be supported in the ante-Nicene Fathers, notably Origen. His interest in Origen has often been noted.[2] Milton was, however, extremely independent, not to say heterodox, in his theological opinions, both in *Paradise Lost* and in the *De Doctrina*. In spite of his Origenistic tendencies, he was too millenarian in his vision of things to come to share Origen's outlook in these matters. The notion of purgatory was clearly repugnant to him: in his charac-teristically Puritan way he accounted it antipathetic to the notion that Christ had purchased full satisfaction for our sins. One there-fore would not expect, nor does one find, any tendencies to re-incarnationism in Milton, though as a student of Jewish kabbalistic lore he must have been familiar with presentations of such views in forms other than those Platonic ones with which he was of course acquainted. Nevertheless, when he is not being consciously theological, for instance, in one of his minor poems written on a child's death, he asks:

> Or wert thou that just Maid who once before
> Forsook the hated earth, oh! tell me sooth,
> And camest again to visit us once more?[3]

Coleridge (1772-1834), also a theologically-minded poet, makes similar reflections on hearing of the birth of a son.[4]

Both the Cambridge Platonists in the seventeenth century and the American transcendentalists in the nineteenth were very much disposed to reincarnationist notions. In general, all poets are in-clined to open themselves to any ideas that are at all plausible. One would expect, therefore, to find reincarnationist allusions scat-tered among their writings. That we do find; but we find also much more. From the Renaissance onward, the great poets of a wide variety of European nations, when at their most serious, often enunciate definite preoccupation with reincarnationist belief and sometimes a deep commitment to it. Shakespeare writes:

> If there be nothing new, but that which is
> Hath been before, how are our brains beguiled,
> Which, labouring for invention, bear amiss
> The second burthen of a former child![5]

Dryden, in one of his odes, alludes to transmigrationism more specifically:

> *If thy pre-existing soul*
> *Was form'd at first with myriads more,*
> *It did through all the mighty poets roll*
> *Who Greek or Latin laurels wore,*
> *And was that Sappho last, which once it was before.*

The notion appears also in Addison:

> *Eternity—thou pleasing, dreadful thought!*
> *Through what variety of untried being,*
> *Through what new scenes and changes must we pass!*

The skeptical Voltaire once remarked that since resurrection runs all through nature, being born several times is no more remarkable than being born once, and therefore the doctrine of metempsychosis is neither absurd nor useless. Goethe was steeped in occultist literature: "I am certain," he remarked at a friend's funeral, "that I have been here as I am now a thousand times before, and I hope to return a thousand times." Schiller, Blake, Shelley, Coleridge, Browning and Southey all allude to reincarnationist notions in such a way as to leave us in no doubt that they took them seriously. Wordsworth's lines on pre-existence are well-known:

> *Our birth is but a sleep and a forgetting;*
> *The Soul that rises with us, our life's Star,*
> *Hath had elsewhere its setting,*
> *And cometh from afar.*

When Benjamin Franklin was twenty-two he wrote an epitaph for himself that later, in a variety of versions, became one of the most famous in the nation's history. Likening his body to the cover of an old book, he looks forward to a new life in which the contents of the book will appear again in a new and better edition, stripped of the errata that disfigured the earlier one. Poe went so far as to write: "It is mere idleness to say that I had not lived before—that the soul has no previous existence." The American poets Longfellow and Lowell, Whittier and Whitman, all show an interest in and sympathy for reincarnationist notions. Whitman cherished very definite beliefs about karma and metempsychosis, which are vividly expressed in *Leaves of Grass* first published in 1855. Flaubert held that heredity is a true principle falsely applied: our real heredity comes from previous existences.

So widespread, indeed, is preoccupation with the reincarnationist theme that it might be easier to make an inventory of poets and novelists who show no interest in it than to make a list of those who do. Moreover, the writers who do show deep interest in the notion are as diverse in temperament as they are varied in background. Among twentieth century poets two of the most unlike would surely be the Irish W. B. Yeats and the English John Masefield, and both make explicit, each in his own distinctive fashion, a very clear belief in a definite, not to say simplistic, form of reincarnationism such as is part of the ideological furniture of the upanishadic literature of India. Masefield was Poet Laureate and also recipient of the very prestigious Order of Merit. The first stanza of his poem, *A Creed,* is quoted at the opening of chapter I. It is a striking statement of reincarnational belief.

Among non-literary figures, interest in the theme is no less astonishing. Henry Ford categorically affirmed a belief in reincarnation. Famous soldiers have also proclaimed their belief in it. There are some indications that Napoleon entertained the notion. Certainly, in more recent times, both Lord Dowding, Chief of the Royal Air Force Fighter Command in the Battle of Britain, and the American General George Patton were ardent subscribers to reincarnationist beliefs. Less well-known is the explicit profession of belief in reincarnation attributed to Lloyd George who, on his death in 1945, was probably, except for Winston Churchill, the most famous British statesman of the twentieth century. Lord Riddell reports that Lloyd George, recalling his boyhood years, said he had been more afraid of heaven than of hell, for he had pictured it as a place of perpetual Sundays with perpetual chapel services presided over by God who, with the assistance of hosts of angels, would be keeping a close check on attendance. That concept of heaven, he went on to say, made him an atheist for ten years. "My opinion," he declared, "is that we shall be reincarnated." What attracted him to the idea was the notion that justice, not least social justice, would be done through the operation of the karmic law.[6]

Among great nineteenth century American figures, Thoreau and William James represent, each in his own very different way, an American tradition that could not be called religious in any conventional sense. Moreover, their respective outlooks, interests and temperaments, were poles apart. Both express belief in reincarnation. "As far back as I can remember," wrote Thoreau in his journal, "I have unconsciously referred to the experiences of a previous state of existence."[7] Thoreau believed reincarnation to be a deep-rooted instinct of the whole human race. He was among the many who have had a very strong sense of the *déjà-vu,* the experience of "having been there before." William James, one of the most notable figures in the history of American philosophy, confesses, in his postscript to his widely-read book, *The Varieties of Religious Experience,* that so far as he could claim to understand the karmic law in Buddhism, he agreed with it in principle.[8]

It was William James's younger brother Henry, a renowned Anglo-American novelist, who suggested to Axel Munthe the writing of the latter's immensely popular memoirs, *The Story of San Michele.* More than once in these memoirs are to be found hints at a reincarnationist outlook. For example, he writes of an old fisherman in Capri whose ways of expressing himself, and sometimes even his very words, were "pure Greek." Munthe whimsically surmises that the old man remembered them from the time he had sailed down that very coast as a member of the crew of Ulysses.

Both George Eliot and her French contemporary George Sand indicate an inclination toward reincarnationism. Among English Victorian women writers, Marie Corelli enjoyed an extraordinary popularity and is said to have been a favorite author of Queen Victoria's. Her novels are saturated with the reincarnationist theme.

REFERENCES AND NOTES

[1]Thomas Browne, *Religio Medici,* XV (London: Chapman and Hall, Ltd., *n.d.*), p. 28.

[2]*See,* for example, H. F. Robins, *If This Be Heresy: A Study of Milton and Origen* (Urbana: University of Illinois Press, 1963).

[3]John Milton, "On the Death of a Fair Infant Dying of a Cough". In *The Poetical Works of John Milton* (Glove edition) (London: Macmillan and Company, 1880), p. 480.

[4]On Coleridge's interest in reincarnation, *see* a paper by Irene H. Chayes, *Journal of English Literary History,* December, 1958.

[5]*The Sonnets of William Shakespeare* (Mount Vernon: The Peter Pauper Press, 1938), p. 59.

[6]*Lord Riddell's Intimate Diary of the Peace Conference and After* (London: Victor Gollancz, 1933), p. 12.

[7]Entry for July 16, 1851. In *The Journal of Henry D. Thoreau* (Boston: Houghton Mifflin, 1949).

[8]William James, *The Varieties of Religious Experience* (New York: Doubleday, Dolphin Books, n.d.), p. 467.

VII

WHICH IS THE SELF?

*There is indeed another, different soul,
called* bhūtātman.

Maitri Upanishad

The contemporary inquirer, accustomed to psychological discussions about the nature of the psyche and to philosophical doubts about the notion of the self, is likely to raise the question: what exactly is it that is supposed by reincarnationists to be reborn? In this chapter we are not to be concerned with the modern philosophical objections: these will be treated in the next chapter. For the present let us consider what in fact those who take reincarnation seriously presuppose the answer to be.

Reincarnationist views have been held by so many diverse peoples and in such varied cultural circumstances that one cannot expect a simple answer to the question. Yet there are certain common tendencies in all reincarnationist thought. For instance, even apart from metaphysical and theological presuppositions, the reincarnationist must see the self that is reborn as other than the self I commonly have in mind when I say "myself" and "yourself". When I talk of "myself" I ordinarily refer to the whole person you recognize as me, including the timbre of my voice, the curve of my eyebrows, and even some features you are less likely to know about, such as a damaged toe. On reflection, however, I must admit that some features of the self I so talk about are ephemeral even by the most ordinary reckoning, such as a back-

70

ache, or a pimple on my neck. They may be with me as I talk to you today but not, I am hoping, when I see you again tomorrow. Even by this ordinary reckoning, therefore, the self is not entirely constant. When I appear before you with some very unusual feature such as a rash all over my face, you may even pause for a moment before recognizing me; but then you will say something such as: "Say, what has happened *to you?*" To say something of that sort is to acknowledge that the self I take to be me and that you recognize as me has undergone a change, but a change that is, all shocks and surprises notwithstanding, superficial. You see, so to speak, below the rash to the "real" self that still has the same kind of smile, the same kind of look of dismay, the same vocal resonance. Even a dramatic increase in my weight or an alarming loss of it would not cause my friends to say: "Who are you?"

The reincarnationist must plainly carry this way of perceiving the self much further. The question is: how much further? All of us, unless we are crass materialists, understand what it means "to see behind" the wrinkles and the injuries to what we may call in a general, poetic sort of way, the "soul" of the person in question. Perhaps the poor man has suffered a stroke that has paralyzed his face and body, and that he has also undergone a tracheotomy, so that he speaks only in a hoarse whisper quite unlike the rich baritone I remember in him. Yet I say, especially if I love or admire the man, that despite all these misfortunes he is "still the same old Bob." I "see" something in him that is, as I might say, still the same, "deep down." In that "deeper" self I may find his old sense of humor, for instance, and his memories of past events we have witnessed together. So, after all, I take Bob to be still "himself".

We must now ask: how much of Bob would have to be taken away before he would no longer be recognizable as Bob, until, perhaps, he no longer *was* Bob? Such a question might well arise in the sphere of medical ethics. Suppose that Bob, in addition to all his other troubles, had lost his mind to such an extent that he became, as people often say in such sad circumstances, "just a vegetable." Legally and ecclesiastically, the miserable remains of Bob that were still living and breathing would still be designated as had been Bob in his prime; but the self that Bob's friends had known and loved would have become indiscernible. Reincarnationists would say, of course, that his "inner" self, the self that had passed through many incarnations and would pass through many more, could not have vanished, for that inner self in every man is indestructible. What is that "inner" self supposed to be and how is it distinguished from other selves that I might call "myself"?

When a great king asks the wise Śākāyanya for spiritual direction, the latter advises him to become a "knower of the soul (ātman)." "This one, assuredly, indeed," he says, "is your own self (ātman)."

"Which one is it, Sir?" asks the king.

Śākāyanya then goes on to speak of the soul (ātman) as immortal, "he who, without stopping the respiration, goes aloft and who, moving about, yet unmoving, dispels darkness." That, he tells the king, is the wisdom "contained in all the Upanishads." The human body, he says, quoting another spiritual discourse, is but "a cart without intelligence (a-cetana)." The soul, by contrast, abides in lonely grandeur: the soul is "pure, clean, void, tranquil, breathless, selfless, endless, undecaying, steadfast, eternal, unborn, independent. He abides in his own greatness."

When, however, the glorious nature of ātman has been expounded, we learn that "there is still another, different one." This is the bhūtātman, "he who, being overcome by the bright or the dark fruits of action, enters a good or an evil womb, so that his course is downward or upward, and he wanders around, overcome by the pairs of opposites." This may be called "the elemental soul." This "elemental soul" is in the grip of matter (prakṛti) and bewildered by its snares. As a bird binds itself with the snare that has caught it and from which it struggles to disentangle itself, so the "elemental soul" becomes more and more overcome by the body that has imprisoned it. Because of its attachments, it is trapped: that is why it returns again and again into other wombs.[1]

Here are very clearly seen the underlying presuppositions of the upanishadic sages. The inmost self (ātman), were it not so ensnared in the empirical world, would never have to go on seeking new wombs. It would have no need to do so. Realizing its own identity with brahman it would dwell serene, for ever free of the loathsome web that is the body. Lest anyone suppose that I exaggerate the hatred of the body that is characteristic of the upanishadic tradition, I cite the text: "Now, it has elsewhere been said: 'This body arises from sexual intercourse. It passes to development in [the darkness of the womb]. Then it comes forth through the urinary opening. It is built up with bones; smeared over with flesh; covered with skin; filled full with feces, urine, bile, phlegm, marrow, fat, grease, and also with many diseases. . . .' "[2]

So what is reborn under the law of karma is not the pure, unadulterated *ātman* but, rather, the self that is intertwined with and crushed under the dead weight of the matter of an alien world, the world of *maya*. From the standpoint of one who has achieved unity with the Eternal (*brahman-ātman*), what a wretched hybrid must be that reincarnating self! It would seem to be, *sub specie aeternitatis,* like an ugly bluebottle hopping from one animal excrement to another. So, indeed, it would go on for ever, but for the merciful though inexorable law of karma, which ensures that sooner or later this hybrid self will tire of its disgusting journey and let the divine within it escape from the karmic law by transcending it. Westerners, when they criticize the Hindu way of life, tend to lament its seeming tendency to perpetuate poverty. That is, of course, to miss the point. From the standpoint of such Hindu classics, which reflect one of the most basic presuppositions of Indian thought, the womb of a princess is as much the enemy of the soul's freedom as is that of a pariah. Both, however, serve under the eternal moral law, the karmic law, being therefore, each equally, the instrument of salvation as well as an obstacle to it. Such a mind-body dualism is deeper than most Westerners readily understand. It is rooted in a very ancient archetype of thought, arising from the primitive discovery of the stupendous powers of the mind, and of the different nature of these powers, as compared with the feebler powers of the body. The denigration of the body thus becomes a primary duty of the spiritually regenerate man and a fundamental article of religious belief.

I am not suggesting that there is anything reprehensible about the process of thought that ends in such a conclusion. On the contrary, it is a valiant attempt to defend an important vision of the human mind as it evolves. It rests, however, on an ancient mistake, namely, the notion that the "real me" is identical with God, its misadventures in the realm of matter notwithstanding. We have already seen that the biblical view is incompatible with that upanishadic one. Moreover, when we ask for a resolution of the problem that we undertook at the outset of the present chapter to examine, the upanishadic view issues in no satisfactory answer. More than the pure *ātman,* eternal and divine, is driven to rebirth; yet the self that is reincarnated cannot be the self that I am at this very instant, since that includes, as we have seen, peculiarities that will not be there even tomorrow, let alone in another incarnation.

At this none will boggle; but we are still to be faced with nonsense. The self that is to be reborn cannot include the maleness of my sexual nature that permeates my whole humanity, since presumably I might be, instead, a woman or a eunuch in my next incarnation, if not the inhabitant of a distant planet in which the reproductive arrangements are unimaginably different. Even my memory, which provides me with the chief instrument by which I have transcended my animal nature and assumed the dimension that makes me a human being, must also go; otherwise I should be able in my next life to remember clearly at least something of my present one. That (despite some cases claimed to the contrary) does not happen, or, if it ever does, its occurrence is very unusual.[3] Having stripped myself as one would an artichoke, I may expect to reach at last an unstrippable core that I can call my inmost self. This core, however, even if I could find it, is not, after all, exactly what is to be reincarnated. For the innermost "me" is eternal and divine, pure and untrammelled, while that which is to be reborn is a less noble self, a self so entangled in the web of futile desires and vain ambitions that it eclipses and envelops the eternal self that lies hidden within it as a last healthy cell lies embedded in a group of cancerous ones. What, then, can this self be that is neither my eternal soul, my *ātman,* nor anything that anyone could ever recognize as me?

A major difficulty in understanding how the ancient mind worked on questions of this kind is that it could be both extremely subtle on some matters and also unimaginably simplistic on others. So we are misled into supposing, on the one hand, that because they knew nothing of computers or even telephones they must have been primitive in all their thought, and, on the other, that because they were obviously highly developed in certain skills they must have been skillful at everything. We cannot easily grasp how such clever people could be so simplistic in the very matters we understand best. They could talk, for instance, of the soul as an "essential self" and as an entity within the body, animating it. They could propound ingenious theories of its having several concentric cells, one within the other. They could speak glibly of its being tangled as a rock might be entangled in seaweed. While some of us may see that they were indeed trying to express a very important truth in that way, we cannot today think like that about the self. The philosophical and scientific reasons against such conceptualization will be considered in the next chapter. For the moment let us simply note that whatever the self is it is certainly no more a blob inside a body than my personality is an organ like my liver. If, then, we wish to defend the notion of man as a "spiritual" being, we cannot do it the way the ancients did it. The self, whatever the term designates, is curiously volatile. I can wipe out whole areas of myself that I had taken to be inseparable from all that is called "me" and yet retain a vigorous sense of my identity. Yet the self seems to remain unfathomable. The term is, to say the least, ambiguous. How could I so empty myself as to leave nothing for my friends to recognize as me, yet re-enter another womb and live again? What can it mean to say "I" might so live again?

REFERENCES AND NOTES

[1]"Maitri Upanishad", 2 and 3. In R. E. Hume, *The Thirteen Principal Upanishads* (London: Oxford University Press, 1921), p. 414.

[2]Ibid., "Maitri Upanishad", 3.4.

[3]*See*, for example, Ian Stevenson, M.D., "The Evidences of Survival from Claimed Memories of Former Incarnations". In *Journal of the American Society for Psychical Research*, LIV, April, 1960, pp. 51-71.

VIII

PHILOSOPHICAL AND
SCIENTIFIC OBJECTIONS

> *My destructive purpose is to show that a
> family of radical category-mistakes is the
> source of the double-life theory. The repre-
> sentation of a person as a ghost mysteri-
> ously ensconsed in a machine derives from
> this argument.*
>
> Gilbert Ryle, *The Concept of Mind*

The marked revival of interest in reincarnationist views that has
occurred in recent years has displayed itself both at a popular level
and in circles devoted to serious parapsychological inquiry.
Psychical research and parapsychological investigation are naturally as suspect among traditionally-minded Christians as is dogmatic theology among those who incline to the notion that inquiry
into the chemistry of the spirit can be just as legitimate as any other
kind of scientific investigation. The theologians tend to view the
parapsychologists and psychical researchers as neo-Gnostics, as
pseudo-scientists parading a merely superficial and false sophisti-
cation. The parapsychologists look on the theologians as so wed-
ded to traditional, not to say petrified, revelations that they have
lost the capacity to receive any new spiritual disclosure, or indeed
to do any creative thinking of a genuinely religious character.

Both sides are exposed, however, to the same objection from

contemporary philosophy and science. The objection is a radical one. It is not directed particularly at any speculation about a "life beyond." It is, rather, an objection to the notion of a "soul" or "spirit" that is supposed to inhabit the body and to be in some way distinct from it. Gilbert Ryle, in an influential book, *The Concept of Mind,* warned philosophers several decades ago against unconsciously accepting such presuppositions, which he took to be an unfortunate legacy from Descartes. Ryle's celebrated gibe about the soul's being "a ghost within a machine" reflects, however, an outmoded view of the state of affairs. For the universe is anything other than a machine, nor is man, who is its microcosmic counterpart. Contemporary positivistic philosophers notoriously often betray their own mechanistic and therefore outmoded scientific presuppositions. The objection, however, comes not only from such philosophers, but no less from religiously-minded scientists such as Teilhard de Chardin who, under a very different motivation, proposes to talk, not of a soul, but of radial energy.[1] Energy is one; but there are two layers of it, the *within* and the *without.* Long ago, Marx's mentor, Ludwig Feuerbach, had punned, *Der Mensch ist was er isst:* man is what he eats. Teilhard recognizes that man must eat in order to think. "But," he discerningly adds, "what a variety of thoughts we get out of one slice of bread!"[2]

What is the nature of the fundamental objection to the notion of a "soul" that has become so obvious to modern philosophical understanding and scientific thought? It cannot be merely that the notion is a primitivistic one, though that is certainly true. For the notion of a universe was also primitivistic and that notion, though of course transformed, is discarded by neither modern philosophers nor modern scientists. We have not rejected astronomy or biology, though we have made enormous methodological advances on them since the days of the Babylonians and of Aristotle respectively. The basic objection to the notion of a "soul" is that even among educated and reflective people, to say nothing of the masses, we find a hangover of that primitivistic way of looking at the "soul", such as vitiates all our thinking, but especially all speculation, theological or theosophical, about survival after death. The very notion of "survival after death" is seen as an absurdity arising from the general category-mistake about the mind-body problem, namely, that there is a body and a mind that are separable from one another as the yolk and white of an egg are separable in the hand of a competent cook. Before we can adequately answer the question raised at the beginning of this paragraph, we must see more precisely what the primitivistic view was.

In primitive societies the notion of the "soul" as a separate and encapsulated entity inhabiting the body as a cherry stone inhabits the cherry, took various forms. It had, however, common characteristics. The Hebrews called it *nephesh,* having in mind a primitivistic notion long antedating the Bible, in which the *nephesh* was conceived as a miniature of the physical person we see, and constructed out of the same "stuff" as the body of that person, only much finer. It was so fine that it could slip out of the nostrils at death unnoticed or, in the case of a violent death, on the point of the assassin's sword. Indeed, sometimes it could slip away during sleep; hence the old superstition, already noted, against sleeping with one's mouth open, so facilitating such wanderings of the soul. When a person goes insane we still say he has "lost his mind," a hangover, of course, from the old concept of the *nephesh.*

In the Book of Ezekiel we find an echo of this primitivistic belief. "Trouble is coming to the women who sew frills around wrists, who make veils for people of all sizes, the better to ensnare lives. . . . Well then, the Lord Yahweh says this. We shall see about these frills you use for snaring lives like birds. I am going to rip your veils to pieces and rescue my people from you; they will no longer be fair game for you. And so you will learn that I am Yahweh."[3] The passage strongly suggests fear of the witches who, in primitive societies, made a profitable business out of nocturnal exploits during which they made off with the *nepheshim* of unwary sleepers, caught them in handkerchiefs or wide sleeves or frilly cuffs, as one might catch caterpillars or moths, and then sold them to families who had among them a person who had "lost his mind." Anthropologists report that similar practices are still attributed to sorcerers in primitive societies today.

The Arabs called the soul *nefs* and entertained similar views about it. The early Greeks also thought of the soul as animating the body. They called it the $\psi \nu \chi \acute{\eta}$, whence, of course, is derived a whole family of modern terms such as "psychology". To what extent Socrates accepted, rejected, or wished to modify such a notion is disputable; but there can be no doubt that the general notion of a soul distinct if not separable from the body was characteristic of the climate of thought in which Socrates and Plato emerged. So the myth of reincarnation, whether the Greek philosophers took it seriously or not, did not raise among them or their listeners the *kind* of objection that would be obvious among us today. In Egypt, a grander and more ancient civilization than that of the Hebrews, a more complex account of the soul was given, comprising, for instance, the *ba* and the *ka*. Nevertheless, the basic presupposition was the same: the soul can detach itself from the body. The *ba*, sometimes depicted as a human-headed bird, resided in the heart or belly and flew from the body at death. The *ka*, however, took up residence in the lifelike statue or representation of the deceased that Egyptian funereal custom prescribed, while the *ba* returned to the body from time to time, provided that suitable arrangements had been provided, which included, of course, mummification and a tiny chimney or passageway to give access and egress for the *ba*. Those who know anything at all about the history of early Indian thought will recognize the same sort of pattern in the metaphysical and religious presuppositions of the *Vedas* and the *Upanishads*. Complex as the notion of layers of selfhood became, the basic notion remained of a self that is somehow or other detachable from its material covering as is the apple seed from the apple. Of course theories of the transmigration of the soul do not *follow* from any such presuppositions; but presuppositions of this kind do make reincarnation plausible. To say the least, they provide a climate of thought that is as hospitable to reincarnationist views as to any other theories of personal immortality. This type of view about the soul was remarkably prevalent in the Mediterranean world. "What shall it profit a man if he gain the whole world and lose his own soul?"[4] The soul can be lost, it seems, and, according to a later development in Latin theology, certain grave sins can so affect it that it is "killed"; that is why such sins are called "mortal". To die in a state of mortal sin is to die with one's soul permanently put out of God's reach. Despite the strongly Hebrew character of Paul's thought, which seems to lead him to a theory of conditional resurrection, the typical Mediterranean presuppositions pervade the New Testament. The soul is the valuable part of the individual. The soul cannot hope to get a "glorified" body at the Resurrection unless it is somehow able to "survive" the present body that is its habitation and so achieve resurrection "in Christ".

It is precisely at this notion of "survival" that contemporary thought boggles. "To survive" means "to live on" and so one naturally asks: what can it mean to say that John died yet continues to live? Either he did not "really" die or else he could not have continued to live. The old answer, grounded in the presuppositions we have discussed, was of this sort: John's body died, but his soul, being immortal, lived on, in one way or another. We must now look more closely at the reasons why contemporary thought finds that kind of answer meaningless, despite the fact that the pre-suppositions on which it is based have flourished since the time of Neanderthal man, as archaeological evidence attests.

The reason why contemporary philosophers find such answers meaningless is that they see very well how, in the history of ideas, the cleavage between a "natural" and a "spiritual" world arose and was developed. It arose because people noticed that the mind functions differently from the body; the "inner life" of a man operates in ways quite unlike his animal life. The existence of neither the one nor the other could be denied, so one tended to say, in effect: there are two worlds, each operating according to different "laws". As mechanical science developed, intelligent people saw they had to take note of it and somehow fit it into a general system of thought. The easiest way to do so was to extend the already existing arrangement while preserving the original dichotomy. The "spiritual" world had a different set of causes behind it from those that affected the mechanical world. Some of the movements of my arms and legs are, on this view, due to mechanical causes, that is, to movements of particles of matter, while other such movements of my limbs arise from movements of my mind. Yet thinkers, in attempting this solution of the mind-body problem, tended to suppose that the laws governing the operations of the mind must be somehow *analogous* to the laws governing the mechanical world. Much as primitive man had seen the soul as modelled on the body (the microcosmic replica to which we have already referred), so the nineteenth century idealist thinkers, confronted with the mechanistic theories of the age of Newton, were inclined to borrow the physicists' models of the "material" world for the construction of metaphysical theories about the "mental" world. The result was somewhat as if one were to conceive of biology as a different *kind* of physics: then one would expect to find a system of biology describable in terms of the physicist's vocabulary, based on his conceptual models and using his relational arrangements. Many contemporary positivistic phi-losophers, indeed, have never entirely overcome that tendency to use Newtonian models in their thinking. That is fatal not only to accurate analysis but also to creative scientific progress. As Max Planck observed, the methods of the positivists, with the kind of verificational criteria these methods demand, could never have permitted the discovery of modern quantum physics. There is plainly something profoundly wrong with methods that would exclude the possibility of such an epoch-making discovery.

The objection from the side of modern science, which has been revolutionized by quantum physics, is no less pointed. Whatever we are to make of the mind-body problem, we cannot hope to deal with it on classical lines. Modern science can provide no haven for the old dualism in any of its forms, primitivistic or otherwise. Herein lay, indeed, much of the genius of Berkeley, who saw in his own way, even in the eighteenth century, that the traditional mind-body dualism simply would not do. Whatever the terms "mind" and "matter" represent, they cannot refer to two distinct "realms" or "worlds". To talk of a "moral" universe and a "physical" one as though the one were sitting on top of the other, or alongside the other, or even interpenetrating the other, is meaningless. This conclusion has been driven home largely because of the modern scientific concept of "field". "A new concept appears in physics," wrote Einstein, "the most important invention since Newton's time: the field. It needed great scientific imagination to realize that it is not the charges nor the particles but the field in the space between the charges and the particles which is essential for the description of physical phenomena. . . . The theory of relativity arises from the field problems. . . . The theory of relativity changes the laws of mechanics. . . . A further consequence . . . is the connection between mass and energy. Mass is energy and energy has mass. The two conservation laws of mass and energy are combined by the relativity theory into one, the conservation law of mass-energy."[5] "Matter", in the light of relativity theory, becomes a name for "that which scientists are trying to understand," so that the view proposed by Berkeley, two centuries before Einstein's work, was much more to the point than even the sympathetic among his contemporaries could have perceived.

Consciousness, then, comes to be seen as energy too, a special development of energy, if you will, but not a separate realm. *Self*-consciousness, however, is a peculiar development in the evolutionary process, arising with the turning inward of consciousness upon itself, the catching by the mind of its own act and therefore of its own being. The attainment of self-consciousness, entailing the development of an inner life, is the most important event in human history and, indeed, in the history of everything the sciences can tell us anything about. This is not, however, because a new "realm" or "world" has been discovered but, rather, because an individual has realized himself as a focus of that energy apart from which nothing can emerge into being.

On the one hand, then, is that movement toward self-consciousness. On the other, however, is the familiar Second Law of Thermodynamics, according to which some of the energy in the universe is eventually dissipated into what we may call a cosmic waste-basket. Such entropy, as the physicists call it, appears to be the opposite pole of the energy process. The consequences of this view of the nature of all things, "mental" or "material", are fatal to the traditional "soul-stuff" theories of immortality. That a part of me, such as has been traditionally called my soul, should survive my body intact, as a cherry stone survives the cherry after the latter has decayed and has been trampled into the ground, becomes inconceivable. The objection is fatal not only to reincarnationist theories *in the form in which they have been generally canvassed* but to *all* notions of personal immortality built upon the same model of an independent soul. With the dynamic view of the universe that modern science takes, nothing can be as static as the soul was presented in traditional models. If whatever is called the soul is to have the importance attributed to it by those who would contend for its immortality, then it must be dynamic *par excellence* and therefore subject to entropy in an eminent degree. So the person I now am, filled with my particular memories, shaped by my peculiar angularities, steeped in my male sexuality, and aglow with the special hopes and fears that play so large a part in defining "me", cannot conceivably survive "as is."

Then is there anything of "me" that could survive? Here we must be quite clear that we are not concerned at this point with whether any such survival of the body does in fact occur. We are not seeking any sort of "proof" or "disproof" of immortality, let alone of reincarnational forms of it. The preliminary question we have to raise just now is simply: is there any account of personal immortality or resurrection that would make sense, whether true or false?

I think there is. Nevertheless, that "self" cannot survive that would include, for instance, my present hopes and fears, my habits of mind, my capacity for speaking certain languages and incapacity for others, my nostalgic sentimentalities and my masculine attitudes, my taste for architecture and my distaste for bridge. All these specificities must perish with the brain and body that have made possible their development in their present forms. Perhaps some *tendencies* might continue, however, such as might connect my present activities with future ones on this or some other planet. Of course, physical reliques of "me" may survive for a time, for example in my writings; but eventually (be it after a million years) entropy will overtake all human artefacts, including the Parthenon and the Sistine Chapel, the last microfilm copy of *Hamlet* and the last score of *Faust*. For these are but petrified recordings and representations of human energy. There is no reason in science or in religion to suppose that any such petrifactions, however precious they be to our hearts, should survive the inexorable entropy at work in the universe. To suggest that there might be a place for them in either a Buddhist nirvana or a Christian heaven is a paradigm of absurdity. Yet hardly less absurd must be the notion that I could carry over my present personality, with all the quirks that please my friends and annoy my foes, and transplant it, either through resurrection or through reincarnation, into another body. No, whatever is supposed to be resurrected or reincarnated must be other than that.

I am no less convinced, however, than is Teilhard that, entropy notwithstanding, the hope of personal survival is well grounded. Having recognized the principle of entropy, we need not go on to assume that the self-conscious energy that is man's "within" cannot escape it. The presumption to the contrary that is characteristic of the thought of many physicists springs from a hidden presupposition that the universe has no energy-fount such as that to which religious people give the name "God". Such an energy-fount, if there be one, must of course survive all entropy, being by definition exempt from it as the spring is exempt from the fortunes of the stream whose source it is. But if the self-consciousness or "within" of man is a development that makes man, however feebly, reflect something of the nature of the energy-fount (as is the understanding of man in Genesis: the *imago Dei*), then escape from entropy cannot seem an impossible human destiny. That is the crux of the whole question: if you do not interpret the universe as having such an energy-fount and the *kind* of purpose that ensues from it, then *of course* there is nothing that could escape entropy. If you do so believe, then, while you will not necessarily reach all

Teilhard's conclusions (I, for one, do not), you will join with him in
seeing why escape from entropy is possible for man.

According to modern (that is, post-Einsteinian) physics, the
classical distinction between energy and matter must be discarded.
We must now say that there is no radical distinction between
energy and mass. Energy has mass; mass represents energy. That
is why we can no longer talk, as did the classical thinkers, of a
spiritual or supernatural realm or substance, contradistinguished
from a material or natural one. Nevertheless, mass is not simply
energy, nor energy simply mass. Energy is mass "spread out"; but
what a difference the "spreading out" makes! A healthy man of
average size weighs less than two hundred pounds, less than a
small horse, and a mere speck compared to the Rock of Gibraltar.
Yet consider what he can do and what he is. How qualitatively
different from a horse or a rock he has become! The complexity of
the human organism is far more wonderful than the psalmist could
have imagined when he praised God "for the wonder of myself."[6]
In man energy is so peculiarly developed and deployed that it is as
if man had found the secret staircase to his own source, having
learned just the right distance at which to stand away from that
source and turn toward it in such a way as to draw to himself
something of the divine immortality. Here indeed lies humanity's
great temptation on making this discovery, the temptation so well
exploited by the serpent, according to the Genesis story, in his
promise to Eve: "you will be like gods."[7] The more profoundly
man attains self-awareness, the more he sees both his likeness and
his unlikeness to God. By no means is he the energy-fount of the
universe; yet, unlike it as he is, he has come to share through it an
escape-hatch from entropy to immortality.

The difference between the ancient "soul-stuff" notion of personal immortality and the one I am proposing is enormous. On the
ancient view, I *am* an immortal soul temporarily clothed in a
human body; on my view, I *have become* a "soul" through millions of years of evolutionary development and struggle, and the
"soul" I have become is capable of immortality. Throughout the
earlier stages of my evolutionary development I was entirely dependent on genetic factors for my inheritance of personal qualities.
At the point at which I became human I attained the capacity to
transcend biological processes to the extent of being able to move
from one incarnation to another. That something very special in
evolutionary history occurred in me when I became human is well
recognized by thinkers of very varied opinions. Cassirer saw the

evolutionary leap as the acquisition of the power to use symbolific language. The Bible tells of God's having breathed into man in such a way that, by the divine *ruach,* man became "a living soul." Whatever symbolism we use, we are forced to recognize that a tremendous leap, leading to a qualitatively novel development, occurred at that point in evolution.

On the view I am tentatively proposing, a biological ancestor of mine *won* the capacity for immortality on becoming human. Whenever I emerged as actually exercising the capacity to be reincarnated, I became to that extent able to transcend my biological history. That does not mean, of course, that I no longer have a biological history. Of course I have. I "take after" my paternal grandfather in this trait and my maternal grandmother in that. I have my father's quick temper and my mother's pride, and so forth. Yet besides being a biological descendant, as have been my ancestors for millions of years, I am now *also* independent of them in the sense that I have a character that is of my own making both in this and in previous lives. I have been subject to the limitations of a thousand wombs. I have been to a thousand schools and escaped from a thousand prisons. Yet with every incarnation, so far as I have improved what the orientals call my karma, I have become more of a person, not merely in the sense of having special characteristics inherited through the inheritance of certain genes, but in the sense of having become, by my own efforts in appropriating the grace of God, more of a personal spirit in my own right. By that I do not mean, of course, in my own right apart from God: I mean in my own right apart from my biological ancestry.

Such growth in the capacity for an actualization of personal immortality is attended by a specific kind of spiritual awareness. It is the kind of awareness that makes people who have it sensitive to religious stimuli and conscious of the presence (and, not less, the absence) of God. It also entails intensified awareness of myself as having an involutionary "within" as well as an evolutionary "without". I am a citizen of two countries: that of my family, with all the genetic inheritance it has conveyed to me, and that of the other "kingdom" to which I belong, in which I participate, by the grace of God, in the attainment of immortality *through* repeatedly victorious resurrection. These resurrections within the reincarnational process are both educative and victorious. To use theological language, they are both a submission to purgatory and a participation in heaven.

The ancients, with their notion of humanity as a special creation, could not see immortality in that way. But they saw in their own way the basic issue. Origen and the other *pre-existiani* in the early Church saw it, as did the vast number of poets and thinkers in the West who adopted a more patently Pythagorean reincarnationism. They thought of man as a "spark of the divine fire" or, if wary of the pantheistic tendencies of such language, they saw him as created immortal because he was created "in the image of God." Their formulations of the notion of personal immortality were therefore, from the standpoint of contemporary philosophy and scientific thought, misguided. Nevertheless, they were grasping in their own way, limited as they were by the knowledge of their day, as is every generation, for the single most important fact about humanity, namely, that man is above all a spiritual being with the capacity for attaining personal immortality.[8]

The discovery of the "within" dimension of human consciousness is an awesome step in human experience. It is also the most exhilarating step we have ever taken. The discovery is made, moreover, in an infinite variety of ways. To exhibit the peculiarly dramatic nature of the discovery that comes with the awakening of human self-consciousness, I will turn to a source that may seem to some unpromising, the nihilistic and atheistic thought of Jean-Paul Sartre. Sartre finds that human consciousness (Heidegger's *Dasein*) does not "fit" its environment at any point. That is why it suffers anguish (*Angst*) and the *malaise* of being like a spot of oil in a bucket of water or a drop of water in a drum of oil. Death is the supreme manifestation of that absurdity. Sartre has been charged by some with dualistic presuppositions inherited from Descartes; but that is beside the point. The point is that he has seen and vividly portrayed an oddity in the situation that goes beyond what the physicists can tell us. The oddity is this: much of what we call "man" is subject to that same entropy to which all else is subject, including much of what has been traditionally called man's "soul"; yet there is a residue that does not fit. Try as we will to fit it to the universe, it is recalcitrant. If we did not see that, death would not look as odd as Sartre very properly finds it to be. Death does not, in fact, look so very odd to those who have only minimally achieved that human self-awareness. It looks odd only to the extent that the peculiar nature of human self-awareness in its relation to the rest of the universe is apprehended. Human self-consciousness is the consciousness of being turned in the opposite direction, so to speak, from everything else in our experience. It is as if, having been engaged for millions of years in self-expansion, I were suddenly to find myself turned inside out and engaging in self-emptying.

Such startling involutions have occurred at various stages of evolutionary development. One remembers that, in the early days of evolutionary theory, brute force seemed at first to be the factor that was needed to attain success in the struggle for biological survival: the survival of the fittest, as the popular phrase went. Then came another recognition: while that might be indeed the case up to a certain point, and might be considered, even, the general state of affairs, success in the higher reaches of evolution demanded very different qualities, such as organization and co-operation: the social virtues. While outward-turned, brute-force energy is needed for development, there comes a point where it no longer suffices. Only the energy that is turned "inward" into the mental and moral consciousness will do. The "within"-directed energy develops into a renunciation of energy, as energy has been understood: it is no longer "clout" but the abdication of "clout". If, then, there is an immortal "part" of man, it would seem to lie somewhere in that direction. There need not be any such "part", of course. There *cannot* be any such "part" if there is no energy-fount such as we call God; but if there is such a fount, such personal immortality becomes intelligible.

We may now inquire what kinds of immortality might be explored in terms of such a hypothesis, and consider them with reference to the plausibility or implausibility of the enterprise of reconciling reincarnationism with Christian faith.

REFERENCES AND NOTES

[1] Pierre Teilhard de Chardin, *The Phenomenon of Man* (New York: Harper Torch-books, 1961).

[2] Ibid., p. 64.

[3] Ezekiel 13. 17f. (J.B.).

[4] Matthew: 16.26; Mark: 8.36.

[5] Albert Einstein and Leopold Infeld, *The Evolution of Physics* (New York: Simon and Schuster, 1938), p. 259.

[6] Psalm: 139.14 (J.B.).

[7] Genesis: 3.5 (J.B.).

[8] How this human capacity is realized may be, of course, variously interpreted.

Simone Weil, one of the greatest religious minds of our century, provides a provocative interpretation. She speaks of a "transubstantiation of energy," a notion she develops out of her view that evil, being transmuted into suffering, is thereby overcome. *See* her "New York Notebook" in *First and Last Notebooks* (London: Oxford University Press, 1970), p. 123.

I X

AFTERLIFE IN THE NEW TESTAMENT

Good master, what must I do to inherit eternal life?

Mark 10.17

Someone may ask, "How are dead people raised, and what sort of body do they have when they come back?" They are stupid questions . . . each sort of seed gets its own sort of body.

1 Corinthians 15.35

The thought of the New Testament writers was steeped in the outlook and presuppositions of their Jewish heritage. That Jewish thought itself, however, had been already affected by Greek ideas. Nowhere was the resultant confusion greater than on questions about an afterlife.

The early Hebrews had harbored a vague, primitivistic notion: the dead went to Sheol, a shadowy place or state like the Greek Hades. They were, indeed, simply reflecting an understanding that was common to almost all the thought of the peoples around them, a cosmology in which the universe is pictured as having three levels: heaven above, the underworld (Hades or Sheol) below, and the earth in between. There are inconsistencies in their talk about such matters, of course. Just as people were vague about "up there" in the sky, so they were hazy about "down there" in Sheol. Sometimes the term is used almost synonymously with the grave. Sometimes it is a kind of euphemism for death. Yet there was a place dimly envisioned, a sort of non-world of darkness and dust. In the Akkadian version of the myth of the descent of Ishtar into that underworld, it is described as a dark house, a land of no-return. No one would choose to go there. All would have echoed Homer's sentiments when he says he would rather be a beggar in the present life than a king in the land of shades. In Sheol there is no knowledge, no activity, no thought;[1] nor is there praise of Yahweh.[2] Indeed, so remote is Sheol that the power of Yahweh is exhibited in the affirmation that it reaches even as far as that.[3]

In later Judaism the influence of other ideas appears, and by the time of Christ there is a complex network of them. One such idea had indigenous roots: the notion of paradise. The Greek word παράδεισος (Hebrew pardēs) is a loan-word from the Old Persian pairi-daeza, used to designate an extensive walled park such as one would expect in the estates of a royal palace. The Garden of Eden had been such a place, and the Septuagint version of the Bible translated the Hebrew word for garden (gan), used in Genesis, by παράδεισος. In the later thought of the Hebrews the hope of a return to such a blissful state is natural, and we find, in the centuries just before Christ, a growing distinction: Sheol becomes the place for the wicked, while the righteous are conducted instead to Paradise. Sheol also comes to be distinguished from Gehenna, which in rabbinical thought by the time of Christ had come to be a place of punishment for the wicked. The name "Gehenna" represented the Hebrew word ge-hinnōm, an abbreviation for "the valley of the son of Hinnom," a geographical entity that divided ancient Jerusalem from the hills to the south and west, the modern Wadi er Rababi that joins the Wadi en Nar (the Kidron) at the south of the hill of Zion. Because it had been at one time the site of a shrine where human sacrifice had been offered, it had acquired an evil repute. Gradually it became the locus (or symbol for the locus) of punishment for the wicked. It was "the dump" where evildoers are to be deposited as "trash" and burned like straw.[4]

By the time of Christ, the concept of a final judgment had developed, so that both Paradise and Gehenna could be, and sometimes were, understood as temporary, intermediate states.

Other notions, however, had been introduced into Jewish thought. The origin of the influences that brought them into it is obscure and in any case need not trouble us here. Most notable among these notions was that of resurrection, which appears in the Maccabean period. The Book of Daniel refers to it almost casually, as though it had been a long-standing belief, though all that we know of early Hebrew thought makes incredible such a presumption.[5] References to resurrection to eternal life are abundant in Jewish literature of the period just before Christ, apocryphal, apocalyptic and deutero-canonical.[6] The New Testament writings clearly affirm that a doctrine of the resurrection was held by the Pharisees but neither by the Samaritans nor by the Sadducees.[7] The Jewish historian Josephus confirms that New Testament witness. By the time Paul was writing his letters to the Churches the situation for Christians had changed radically because of belief that Jesus, after his death on the Cross, had been "raised from the dead." Paul and others taught that, *on account of* this supreme demonstration of the power of God in Christ, Christians might expect to be raised *by him and with him* to eternal life.[8] John teaches that "on the last day" Jesus will raise up those who believe in Christ.[9] The promised resurrection is resurrection to a *new* life with a new and glorified body (*soma*). Paul deplores a notion that apparently had been proposed, that the resurrection had already occurred here and now. Such teachings, he warns Timothy, are "pointless philosophical discussions" and corrosive of true faith.[10] Nevertheless, though the Christian hope of resurrection is specifically allied to belief in the resurrection of Christ, the way had already been prepared for the resurrection idea by its development in late pre-Christian Jewish thought. That idea had taken various forms; but what is important for us to notice is the fact that the heritage of the first Christians had accustomed them to think in such terms.

They were by no means accustomed, however, as were some of their Gentile converts, to the notion of that kind of immortality that is found where body and soul are conceived as belonging to separate realms. The Gnostic climate that prevailed, and that became by the second century A.D. a problem for the Church, encouraged such a dualism, introducing into Christianity an element alien to the mainstream of the Jewish tradition that was its heritage. Gentile Christians always found the Old Testament difficult to understand. For many reasons it was alien and mysterious to them, so that, while they formally reverenced it and could appreciate some elements in it, such as the Psalms and the stories of the great heroes of Israel, they were not at all able to make its ideology their own. They inevitably tended, therefore, to transform biblical ideas about the future life into notions more amenable to their own ways of thinking. Both the notion of an immortal "soul-stuff" and of a resurrection were familiar in current mythologies. So, of course, was reincarnation. All such ideas were naturally fused and in other ways commingled in interpreting biblical references to the after-life. We have already seen something of the extent to which re-incarnationist ideas affected the thinking of some early Gentile Christians.

A highly important commingling had already taken place, how-ever, in the thought of the New Testament writers themselves, who were writing in Greek for the whole Mediterranean world. For in their own Jewish heritage lay not only the primitivistic notion of shadowy survival and of resurrection but also the notion of an intensification of life itself. The Hebrews loved life. They could appreciate Deutero-Isaiah's promise that those who hope in Yahweh "put out wings like eagles . . . run and do not grow weary, walk and never tire."[11] What is promised in the New Testament is not surprisingly always described in terms of $life$. The word used is $ζωή$ and the idea of $ζωή$ came from the Old Testament writers. While the early Hebrews had seen "length of days" as the great hope, a more reflective element in Hebrew thought perceived that (as Seneca was to put it in his Stoic way) one should seek not so much to live long as to live well.[12] Quality of life is what must be sought, and this quality is to be found pre-eminently in God, whom the psalmist calls "the fountain of life."[13]

The Greeks used several words for "life". When they wanted to specify the notion of life as a span of time, they used $βίος$, the word from which we get the word "biography". When, on the contrary, they wished to express the notion of life as the vital principle of the body they used the word $ψυχή$, from which we get terms such as "psychology" and "psychiatry". For the notion of life itself, considered in independence of special ideas such as the span or continuum, on the one hand, and, on the other, the vital principle animating the body, they used a word that in the New Testament comes to be the most fundamental one: $zōē$.

In the New Testament, $ζωή$ is the term always used in phrases such as "eternal life", signifying a life that is fuller, richer, and in every way better than the ordinary life we share with cats and dogs. Good as that ordinary life is, it is not to be compared with that richer life that comes from God and is seen as mediated by Christ to those men and women who are mystically united to him by their faith. "The life is more than meat."[14] The paradox is developed in the saying attributed to Jesus: "He that findeth his life shall lose it, and he that loseth his life for my sake shall find it."[15] Notwithstanding Paul's warning to Timothy, just noted, this richer life can be discovered in the present as well as in the future. Jesus hints at this in his ironic aside to those who, on the pretext of duty to attend a funeral, would have delayed following him: "let the dead bury their dead."[16] Similarly, the prodigal son "was dead and is alive again."[17] More dramatically still, the writer of the Fourth Gospel assures us that he who believes in Christ *"hath* everlasting life."[18] He is already in possession of it. Such a person has entered into the inheritance of his everlasting estate. $\zeta\omega\acute{\eta}$ is a notion to which that Evangelist loves to allude. It permeates the Fourth Gospel. When Jesus expounds his doctrine to the woman at the well, telling her that who should drink of the water that he was to provide need never thirst again, he explains that that water should be "a well of water springing up into everlasting life."[19]

In the New Testament is another element, however, well-known to biblical scholars and plain enough even to the most casual reader. We have already perfunctorily noted it. Its importance cannot be overestimated, for despite the fact that we all know about it, we tend to forget how enormously it affected the early Christians, separating their thought from ours and making their whole attitude to life radically different from that which ours ever could be. I refer to the fact that they expected the world as we know it to end *soon,* that is, if not tomorrow, probably within the life-time of at least the younger members of the Christian community. If we but stretch our imaginations to try to grasp what such an attitude did to their whole outlook on questions of the afterlife, we can easily enough see that what seems to us a basic confusion in their thought made sense to them in the light of the urgency they saw in the situation. As they constantly remind themselves, the end of the world is at hand. The world is dying of old age. Men and women have always died (is not death the wages of sin?),[20] and many of Christ's own, those who believe in him and follow him, are to die too, even as did Jesus himself. Nevertheless, they have already in some measure entered into the new life with Christ, and in the impending Day of Judgment they will take full possession of it. Death, therefore, though real, is seen to be a falling asleep for a time. The Catacombs are full of inscriptions to that effect. A brother or sister lies here "asleep in Jesus" and awaiting his coming in glory. They are as much part of the Household of Faith as are they who are still on this side of the veil of death. Some, however, shall not die, for the great Day is to arrive before death overtakes them. Instead of being "raised from" the dead, they will simply answer the call of Jesus, the Great Judge of all men, and enter completely upon the inheritance they have already in some sense begun to enjoy.

That understanding of Christian faith persisted for a long time in early Christian history, and, as we all know, it has had periodic revivals in various millenarian groups. The notion of reincarnation as that notion is understood in upanishadic terms, in association with karmic doctrines, was of course irrelevant to a situation that was so understood. A doctrine of *pre-existence of souls,* however, was not, and no form in which reincarnationist theory presented itself to the minds of Christians in that situation could refer to the future. Reincarnation might have occurred in the past; it could not occur in this world in the future, since there was to be no such world. If people today were generally convinced that the world was coming to an end by, say, the middle of the twenty-first century at the latest, there could be no sense at all in my talking of how my karma would affect my future incarnations on this planet. It would not even be good science-fiction. Moreover, to the first century and second century Christians who expected the world to be "rolled up like a scroll"[21] details of the nature of the life to which Christians were to be raised could not but appear to be idle and foolish conjecture. Christians, in their new life, would be "in Christ" or "with Christ": that was all they needed to know. An orphaned child, if assured of its return to the beloved parent of whom it has thought itself bereft, would not ask, "Shall we live in a house like the one in Ohio or like the one in Tennessee?" No, of course, nothing would matter but the reunion. So, with the daily expectation of the Second Coming of Christ, the early Christians believed that eternal life, whose secret the young ruler had asked of Jesus, not only was now within their grasp but had been already begun in them. That same Jesus who had promised superabundant $\zeta\omega\acute{\eta}$ to his disciples had also told them why he could promise it:[22] he is the source of it. "I *am* the $\zeta\omega\acute{\eta}$."[23] Death, the final and most terrible of all man's enemies, had lost its power. In the lives of

Christians the sting had been taken out of it.[24] They were on their way to join him who in them had begun the infusion of that quality of life they already saw to be eternal. Obviously, the whole question of reincarnation, whether pre-existence had been taken seriously or not, had to be set aside.

By the time the expectation of the Parousia or Second Coming had lost its urgency, having dwindled in status from an existential hope to a theological doctrine, a whole array of Hellenistic notions about immortality and resurrection had been poured into Christian thought. One element in primitive Christian thought, however, which had been there from the beginning and remained after belief in the imminent Second Coming had receded, tended to put reincarnational ideas out of court. When Christians thought of the afterlife, they associated it with death and judgment, and both of these ideas were invested, each in its own way, with a terrible finality. Death was final, the end of the individual as he was on earth. It was the end of his earthly pleasures and pains, hopes and fears. It was the end of him as he was known to himself and to others. Whatever happened to him after death, he was to be changed. So death was a beginning as well as an end. Judgment, too, was final and it was both particular to the individual and general for the human race. It was to be the end of the world and the beginning of a new order, if not the cessation of time itself. So reincarnation, if it could have any place at all, could have only a very limited place in such a scheme of things. Moreover, it must have tended to seem pointless to many of those who considered it at all. As the vision of the Last or Final Judgment confronted people, what difference could lie between one life on earth and a few thousand successive lives? Popular preaching naturally stressed the urgency of the decision that men and women must make: here and now, a decision for all eternity.

Nevertheless, apart from these special circumstances in the Christian climate of thought, there was nothing to exclude the possibility of reincarnation. Theoretically, it could have been squared with either a "soul-stuff" immortality doctrine (as in the mythology adopted by Plato) or a resurrection doctrine. Reincarnation is, of course, a kind of resurrection. Great importance was attached by Christian theologians, however, to the notion of the resurrection of the "same body" that we now have, though in a glorified form. The so-called Athanasian Creed affirms that all men shall rise again with their bodies (*resurgere habent cum corporibus suis*), and a council held at the Lateran against the Albigenses asserted that all shall rise again with their own bodies, *the bodies they now have: omnes cum suis propriis resurgent corporibus, quae nunc gestant.* St. Thomas Aquinas considered that the body that is resurrected must be in some sense the same as the one on earth; otherwise, he thought, one would have to talk, not of a resurrection, but of the assumption of a new body: *nec dicetur resurrectio sed magis novi corporis assumptio.*[25] In the Beatific Vision (the endless state of bliss for the redeemed in Christ), the body one now possesses would be in some way gathered together and in some way transmogrified into a glorious and everlasting body.

All this was conceived, of course, in a climate of now antiquated scientific concepts. Thomas followed Aristotle in his insistence on the unity of body and soul, a philosophical doctrine he could easily christen since it happened to accord, or seem to accord, with the biblical doctrine of man. I do not think what we have seen in the preceding chapter about the nature of energy as it must be understood in the light of modern scientific thought would have radically changed his mind about resurrection, any more than would our modern knowledge of the constantly changing cells of the body that makes me able to say the body I now have is not (from one point of view at any rate) the same as I had ten years ago. Such considerations would have diminished, however, if they would not have entirely eliminated, the need in patristic and medieval thought to insist so stridently on the continuity of the resurrected body. For today we see no "soul" and "body" to be so connected, so that the importance formerly attached by Christian theologians to this question can be eliminated.

In any case, such very Latin teaching about a *carnis resurrectio* does not seem to fit Paul's teaching in the New Testament, which is that the body is to be of a new order, the perfect instrument of the $\pi\nu\epsilon\upsilon\mu\alpha$, the spirit, and, though organized in relation to an identifiable personality, not otherwise recognizable as the same body as the one on earth. The curious notion of the revivification of the material particles of the body does not arise in St. Paul.[26] So many varieties of resurrection theory have prospered within Christian thought, however, that apart from the considerations we have already taken into account, concerning the finality of death and judgment, there would seem to be no fundamental reason why a reincarnation doctrine should not have been admissible.

From early times, but with increasing momentum in the Middle Ages, the doctrine of an intermediate state was developed. That state, which came to be called purgatory, did not mitigate the awful final judgment of eternal bliss in heaven or eternal pain in hell; but it did introduce a dimension that is peculiarly relevant to the reincarnationist view, which, when conjoined to karmic doctrine, is itself a purgatorial scheme. To the development of doctrines of purgatory, therefore, we must now turn our attention in the next chapter, so as to see whether it would be possible to interpret it honestly, from a Christian standpoint, on reincarnationist lines.

REFERENCES AND NOTES

[1] Ezekiel 9.10.

[2] Psalm 6.6.

[3] Deuteronomy 32.22; Psalm 139.8; Amos 9.2; Isaiah 7.11.

[4] 1 Enoch 48.9. Among apocryphal books, Enoch was particularly popular with Christians in the first two or three centuries. It is one of the most important examples of that early apocalyptic literature of which the Book of Daniel is the great prototype. Daniel is the latest of the writings in the Hebrew Bible, dating mainly from about 165 B.C. Enoch, though it incorporates older material, reflects the typical Jewish outlook shortly before the time of Christ.

[5] Daniel 12.2.

[6] See, for example, 2 Maccabees 7.9; 14.46.

[7] Matthew 22.23; Mark 12.18; Luke 20.27; Acts 23.8.

[8] E.g., 2 Corinthians 4.14; Philippians 3.10; 2 Timothy 2.11. Paul expounds his view of the matter especially in 1 Corinthians 15.

[9] John 11.25; 6.39.

[10] 2 Timothy 2.17.

[11] Isaiah 40.31.

[12] Benjamin Franklin echoes this injunction in *Poor Richard*.

[13] Psalm 36.9.

[14] Luke 12.23.

[15] Matthew 10.39; 16.25.

[16] Matthew 8.22; Luke 9.60.

[17] Luke 15.32.

[18] John 3.36.

[19] John 4.14.

[20] Romans 6.23.

[21] Cf. Revelation 6.14.

[22] John 10.10.

[23]John 14.6.
[24]1 Corinthians 15.55.
[25]*Summa Theologiae* 3, supp. 79, 1.
[26]See, for example, 1 Corinthians 15.35.

X

REINCARNATION
AS PURGATORY

> *The soul, so seeing that it cannot, because*
> *of the impediment [in itself], attain to its*
> *end, which is God, and that the impedi-*
> *ment cannot be removed from it, except by*
> *means of purgatory, swiftly and of its own*
> *accord (volontieri) throws itself into it.*
>
> Saint Catherine of Genoa,
> *Treatise on Purgatory*

The particular form of purgatorial doctrine that was developed in
the medieval Latin Church had singularly unfortunate consequences. Not only did it lead to notorious practical abuses and so
contribute to the use of drastic methods of Church reform; it
disastrously obscured the subtler and more interesting understandings of the doctrine within the Catholic tradition itself. Because of the crudity of the later medieval form of the doctrine and
the grave abuses that attended it in practice, the heirs of the
Reformation were often extremely hostile to it. Much worse, however, were its effects in diminishing serious reflection on the whole
notion of an intermediate state. Despite the fact that mystics like
St. Catherine of Genoa (1447–1510) had written beautifully and
incisively on the notion of a purgative state, prejudice against
purgatorial conceptions was very strong indeed in thoughtful cir-

cles, till the nineteenth century, when the Tractarians developed more intelligible accounts of it.

The notion of prayers for the dead goes back at least to the Maccabean period in Judaism. Judas Maccabaeus sent about two thousand drachms of silver to Jerusalem, so that a sin-offering might be made for the Jews, fallen in battle, on whose bodies pagan amulets had been found. That battle occurred in 166 B.C. The account was probably written by a Pharisee in Egypt about forty years later.[1] Yet prayers for the dead, which entail belief in some intermediate state in which their lot may be changed or modified, did not become part of normal synagogue worship till about 130 A.D.

By A.D. 200, however, Tertullian is referring to the practice as standard and well-recognized within the Christian Church. Tertullian is merely noting a state of affairs. He has no vested interest in it. Indeed, he remarks that there seems to be no biblical sanction for it. Both Origen and his teacher, Clement of Alexandria, explicitly propose, however, a doctrine of an intermediate state. They conceive it as a *form* of punishment, though training rather than punishment.[2] It is better understood as purification.[3] Such notions among the Greek Fathers of the Christian Church had their roots, no doubt, in Orphic and other ideas that were part of their general intellectual and cultural heritage. Still, the practice of remembering the dead in prayer was a natural development within the Church. The practice of offering the Holy Sacrifice for the dead is attested in Eastern Fathers such as St. Cyril of Jerusalem and St. Chrysostom as well as by Tertullian. It makes no sense apart from a doctrine of an intermediate state, for there could be no use praying for those whose afterlife could be in no way affected, as would be the case with souls who were already in a final state. Epiphanius goes so far as to account the denial of the efficacy of such prayers for the dead a heresy.[4] The role of prayers for the dead is clearly seen in the Greek liturgies. In contrast to the Latin West, however, the tradition of the Eastern Church was characteristically open, not to say intentionally vague, about the nature and meaning of such references, and has no less characteristically so remained.

The way to a clear enunciation of the much more explicit medieval Latin view of purgatory was opened up by Augustine, who had no doubt learned something of it from Ambrose, his teacher. Ambrose had already asserted that the departed souls await the end of the world in various "habitations", which vary according to their works on earth. Theoretically, that would be compatible with a reincarnationist interpretation. Augustine is more specific: the souls of men are judged immediately on death, and some go at once to a place of purification.[5] A thousand years later, Dante was to give expression in his great epic to that notion, which he poetically presents as a seven-storeyed mountain, each storey providing a place for the purification of a particular one of the seven "deadly" sins. Gregory the Great had also taught that there is an intermediate state in which souls, deprived of the vision of God, wearily await it.

By the time of Thomas Aquinas, purgatory as a place of punishment for those not yet fit for heaven was well established. He could speak confidently of its peculiar pain which is nevertheless mingled with the joy of knowing that heaven is to come. The pain, which is by fire, is, however, terrible: greater than the greatest pain on earth. Naturally, people wished to mitigate the sufferings of their loved ones, so the practice of masses for the dead flourished. The Greeks, who in principle dislike rigorous definition in such matters, objected to the Roman teaching on purgatory. In 1274 the Council of Lyons, and in 1439 the Council of Florence, affirmed only the essential points: there is a purgatorial state, and prayer and other works are efficacious in respect to it. The whole Church was in general agreement on the principle of an intermediate state and on the efficacy of prayers for those who are in it. The Greek Church disapproved only the claim to precise knowledge about it to which the medieval Roman Church seemed to pretend. Eastern Orthodoxy continued to uphold the notion, as it had been expounded from primitive times, and reaffirmed it at the Synod of Jerusalem in 1672.

In the nineteenth century, the English Tractarians, who were in the forefront of the movement to foster the restoration of the plenitude of ancient Catholic doctrine in the English Church, defended the concept of an intermediate state and developed a special form of it. Theological opinion among Anglicans, though it has varied on this as on other subjects, now generally favors the concept of an intermediate state but stresses much less the notion of purification and much more that of development and growth. Views of this sort plainly open the way to an understanding of the intermediate state in terms that more closely resemble what is likely to have been the primitive view of the matter. They also make possible and even plausible, in principle, the interpretation of that state in reincarnationist terms. We shall return to this point later.

The more salutary understanding of purgatory that was developed under Tractarian influence was shared by profound thinkers in the Roman Church of the same period. Baron von Hügel, as a layman of influential family, could be more outspoken during the period (about the turn of the century) when the persecution of "Modernism" was at its height, than could the majority of contemporary Roman Catholic scholars who were priests and therefore more directly subject to ecclesiastical interference. That deeply perceptive thinker, whose influence at the time was greater outside his own Church than within it, did much to show how the customary Roman Catholic presentations of the doctrine of purgatory fell short of, and indeed traduced, the thought of the Roman Catholic Church itself. His studies, in his *opus maximum*,[6] treated especially of St. Catherine of Genoa, to whom we have already alluded and whose thought on the subject surely penetrates much deeper into the noblest of Christian traditions about it.

Catherine was thoroughly medieval in her basic presuppositions, yet prophetically modern in much of her interpretation of traditional doctrine. She accounted the intermediate state purgative but stressed also the purgative character of the present life. Holiness consists, according to her, not so much in the absence of faults as in the presence of creative love in the soul. When a person dies, he recognizes immediately the nature of the impediment that prevents his full enjoyment of God and therefore throws himself instantly and voluntarily into the purgative state. That is because the longing of the soul for that final union with God that theologians call the Beatific Vision in heaven is so great that the soul impetuously seeks the quickest possible way of preparing itself for that final consummation of its joy. The suffering of purgatory becomes, then, an excruciating longing for God, the terrible, burning desire of the soul to fit itself for its final destiny. Were there a quicker way of attaining that end, the soul would surely find it.

As Catherine unfolds her vision, its susceptibility to a reincarnationist interpretation becomes more and more obvious. As we have noted, she sees the soul deciding, immediately on death, what it must do and then instantly, spontaneously doing it. Once it has so acted, however, it cannot withdraw from its decision. In the first instant, it had freedom to choose; thereafter it has abdicated its freedom till the consummation of its purpose. It must submit to the consequences of its own decision. One might almost say that at the instant of death it voluntarily committed itself to a correctional institution but that, having signed the papers, it cannot leave till it has completed its self-imposed sentence. Though in its imprisonment it finds a kind of contentment with the will of God, it also suffers indescribable pain. Yet the pain is the discovery of the obstacles within itself that impede its own progress toward God.

I am not suggesting, of course, that Catherine had a reincarnationist schema in mind. Nevertheless, how well her vision fits a reincarnationist account! On death, the basic "self" or "radial energy" spontaneously moves toward the particular rebirth it needs as a remedy for its state. As it chose to construct the karmic condition in which it now finds itself, so it chooses to work out its karma in the appropriate way. Superficially, it would seem to have no choice; but it has. It *could* choose an even more difficult working out of its plight; but of course it chooses the quickest and best rebirth available, as surely as a cornered fugitive chooses the easiest escape route he can find, with whatever consequences the use of that route entails. Of course there is a predetermined situation in which the soul (to use Catherine's language) has no choice; but such a determinism exists in the background of any intelligible account of the exercise of a free act of the will. Once the soul has entered into another womb at conception, its choice is complete. It must go through with the life it has chosen, with all that life's limitations and woes, with all its self-educational possibilities and self-fulfilling opportunities.

The traditional symbol of purification is fire. According to Catherine, the purgatorial fire consumes all the dross but cannot consume the gold. The gold, once the dross has all been consumed, is impervious to fire. That is, the soul, when completely purified, cannot suffer any more. It can no longer feel the fire. The purified soul finds itself in God; that is, the fire that was so painful in the course of the purifying process now turns out to be what in fact it was all the time: God. The gold has been all the time in the fire, which is God, but while the dross was mixed with the gold, the fire caused suffering; now that the dross has gone it can cause only joy. Catherine's use of such imagery can also lend itself to a reincarnationist interpretation. If the sufferings we endure in life are brought upon ourselves, as the karmic law provides, they only seem to be caused by an external force. As soon as we are cured of the disease that makes us sensitive to the pain, we feel pain no longer. The external circumstances remain the same; it is we who have changed. The medicine tastes ill; I suffer pain and nausea because of it; but as soon as it has effectively done its work I feel only a great sense of well-being in the body that only yesterday writhed in pain. To rid me of the dross might take a million lives, each one a nostrum for a different sort of disease I have brought upon my soul. At last, however, I am completely cleansed, entirely healthy, resistant to every disease to which the soul is subject, and strengthened by successive reincarnations till no harm can come to me. That would be the end of my pilgrimage.

Such, at any rate, would be a conceivable reconstruction of the purgatorial notions of Catherine of Genoa that Baron von Hügel so much admired. Among the Tractarians in the Church of England, however, the tendency to re-interpret purgatory as more a state of growth and development than of punishment for or even purification of sin, is even more promising for a possible reincarnationist understanding of the indubitably ancient Catholic doctrine of an intermediate state.[7] Again I would emphasize the fact that I do not for a moment suggest that such an understanding was much in the mind of these nineteenth century Anglican divines, if it was ever in their minds at all, as a possible interpretation of the meaning of the doctrine of an intermediate state. I think, however, we should consider the possibilities their very plausible view affords for our present investigation. One of the Thirty-Nine Articles of Religion, to which every candidate for ordination in the Church of England was required to subscribe, specifically condemned the "Romish Doctrine concerning Purgatory." It states: "The Romish Doctrine concerning Purgatory, Pardons, Worshipping and Adoration, as well of Images as of Relics, and also Invocation of Saints, is a fond thing, vainly invented, and grounded upon no warranty of Scripture, but rather repugnant to the Word of God."[8] The Tractarians, in interpreting this article, generally held that it referred only to the "Romish" understanding of purgatory, leaving them free to teach an alternative doctrine of the afterlife conceived as a process of growth and development. They were saying, in respect of the "intermediate state", as they preferred to call purgatory, something such as an enlightened modern theologian might possibly say in respect of God: "I renounce the notion that God sits on a throne in the sky, bearded and with sceptre in hand, as in the old iconography; but my renunciation does not in the least entitle you to call me an atheist. On the contrary I am an ardent believer in God."

John Henry Newman, long after he had left the Tractarian movement of which he had been one of the most prominent leaders, and only a few years before he received, in old age, the cardinal's hat from Rome, wrote a memorandum reporting the dream of a Protestant lady the night before she died. She dreamed that her daughter, who had died ten years previously, "appeared to her in shining light, and said, 'Mother, I am permitted by God to come and speak to you before you leave the earth.' She then asked her, 'Are you in heaven? are you happy?' 'Not yet in heaven,' she was answered, 'but O so happy! Busy, busy for God—doing work for him.' The old mother asked what work. 'Not employments as on earth—we see and know so differently,' and she added, 'I cannot tell you more than I am permitted by God.' Her mother asked her if she knew what passes here. She said, 'No, nothing since I left the earth; I remember my own life perfectly, but nothing after.' Then she asked by name after her husband and children, and each of her brothers and sisters. This dream left the lady 'perfectly radiant from henceforth.' At this time she 'seemed quite well.' " Newman goes on to note what an unusual type of dream it seemed to him, especially for a Protestant woman, unlike what would occur even "to most Catholics." "Where," he asks, "did the lady get the ideas which make up this dream?" Having enumerated six points about the dream that he accounted significant, he goes on to say that he was "the more struck with the dream, because I have either long or at least lately, held about the intermediate state all the six points I have enumerated." One of the points was the notion of "employments" in purgatory, on which he mentions he had been lately giving some thought.[9] In a letter written a few months later he writes: "I think what a severe purgatory it would be, tho' there were no pain at all, but darness, silence, and solitude, and ignorance where you were, how you held together, on what you depended, all you knew of yourself being that you *thought*, and no possible anticipation how long this state would last, and in what way it would end. . . ."[10]

Such openness in regard to the nature of purgatory, typical of the liveliest thought in the English Church in the nineteenth century, was carried over by Newman into his Roman period. The notion of an intermediate state in which, after death, the soul goes on to an undesignated place or state in which it has opportunities for further growth and development naturally raises the question: what sort of place might it be, or what sort of state? Reticence on such details was characteristic of the Anglican climate at the time. Moreover, people could then still take seriously the notion of a disembodied soul living on in a "spiritual" world, awaiting the resurrection that would take it at last to heaven. We have seen, however, that one of the greatest of the intellectual gulfs between us and our Victorian ancestors is precisely at this point: we cannot think of the soul in such a way. If, then, we are to consider the notion of an inter-mediate state at all, we ask more importunately than did our forefathers: where? how? It might be on other planets, planets perhaps in other galaxies, but surely it would have to be in a life not *entirely* alien to life on earth. Indeed, we naturally go on to ask: is there any reason why it should not be on earth? At least might not it be in some cases a return to earth rather than another life on Pluto or elsewhere? In other words, the more we raise the old questions about the traditional afterlife themes, the more we are bound to take seriously such possibilities.

All growth entails suffering of one sort or another. We talk of "growing pains"; but the whole educational process, however conceived, and the whole process of growing up, is painful. It is also, however, attended by a joy and an immense satisfaction in the achievement. All this is eminently conformable to what seems to be so universally said of purgatory as anciently conceived: it is an excruciating pain, yet radically unlike the pain of hell, for far from having in it the sense of final, irrevocable loss, it has within it the hope, indeed an assurance of the certainty of final salvation and everlasting bliss. This mixture of struggle and anguish with hope and *joie de vivre* is characteristic of human life. It is a struggle rather than a hymn; yet for many of us it is to the tune of a hymn. It is a vale of tears; yet through the tears is a heavenly vision. How plausible, then, to suggest that purgatory sounds not so very different from life on earth. The old images of heaven and hell are so different from anything we can possibly experience in ordinary life that many people find them inconceivable. Purgatory is in another case. It does not make the same demands on our imagi-nation, or, as some would prefer to say, it does not sound so unintelligible. Some of us occasionally murmur, perhaps half in jest, that we are having our purgatory on earth. With considera-tions such as we now have before us, however, might not that be precisely what is to be said seriously of *all* human life? Might not this life of ours be that "intermediate state", and might not it be a long and evolutionary process far beyond the confines of any one particular span of years, three-score, five, or a hundred and ten?

We need not concern ourselves here with metaphysical and theological questions about the final end of the process, about the ultimate loss of God, the *poena damni* that the classic theologians called hell, or with the baffling puzzles attending the notion of the final state of bliss to which they gave the name of heaven. In such ideas there is plenty of scope for faith: it is wiser for Christians to say simply that to be with God for ever is heaven and to be for ever separated from him is hell. The intermediate state might well be conceived, however, in the concrete terms of reincarnationist teaching.

One of the questions most often asked of protagonists of reincarnationist theories is: why do not we remember past lives? There are certain standard answers; for example, in Vedantist thought only one of seven "selves" is reincarnated (a self at the core of the other selves), and memory is not inseparable from that fundamental self. The Christian could readily see another dimension in such a notion, namely, that deprivation of memory would be essential to new development and new growth, since it is precisely the burden of memory, with all the sense of guilt, all the remorse, all the heartaches from the past, that impede our genuine growth in our later years. No sensible person really expects an octogenarian, however vigorous his body and resilient his mind, to be open to radically new ideas that have been alien to him all his life. For that he would need an entirely fresh start. When we have led a full life, our minds are cluttered with memories; we need a clean slate to make that fresh start. If I were able to remember hundreds of incarnations back to my life as a farmer in Babylonia and including my life as a court jester at the court of Philip the Fair, to say nothing of a brief life in the workhouse in Dickens's England and a tragic life as a Russian princess, you could hardly expect me to bear the burden of it all and still profit from yet another life on earth. Newman's Protestant lady's dream suggests otherwise; but presumably she was not envisaging purgatory in reincarnationist terms, nor was she considering the consequences of carrying the memories of even one life into the life beyond. To grow, one must be young. Youthful at heart though many of us remain, a time comes when no growth is conceivable without a shedding of our memory. Indeed, even in the life we know on earth, one of the greatest mercies is our capacity to forget. But for that merciful ability, we could not endure even one life let alone a succession of them, and eventually we could not but stop making any moral progress at all.

REFERENCES AND NOTES

[1] 2 Maccabees 12.43.

[2] Clement, *Stromata*, 7, 26.

[3] Origen, *De principiis*, 2, 10, 6.

[4] Epiphanius, *Panarion*, 75, 8.

[5] *De Civitate Dei*, 21, 13 and 24.

[6] *The Mystical Element of Religion* (New York: E. P. Dutton and Company, 1908).

[7] Cf. the "Prayer for the whole state of Christ's Church" in the present American Book of Common Prayer, p. 74 f., in which prayer is offered that those who have gone beyond this life may have "continual growth in thy love and service."

[8] *Book of Common Prayer*, "Articles of Religion", Article XXII.

[9] Wilfrid Ward, *The Life of John Henry Cardinal Newman*, Vol. II (London: Longmans Green and Company, 1912), p. 567, (Memorandum, August 29, 1875).

[10] Ibid., p. 568, (Letter, December 4, 1875).

XI

MORAL EVOLUTION

> *For a rational but finite being, the only thing possible is an endless progress from the lower to higher degrees of moral perfection.*
>
> Kant, *Critique of Practical Reason*

Immanuel Kant, the greatest European thinker of his age and one of the greatest philosophers of all time, denied the possibility of formulating any proof of the existence of God by any of the traditional arguments. From "pure" reason one could arrive at no such conclusion, but from "practical" reason one must, he held, make three postulates: God, freedom and immortality. Where metaphysical arguments fail, moral arguments succeed. If we grant the existence of the moral law, and of the *summum bonum* or perfect happiness that is the object of the human will, we are compelled, Kant argued, to acknowledge these postulates (which he accounted the basic ideas of religion), since without them we could not maintain the necessary causal relations between the moral law and the *summum bonum* or perfect happiness that is its goal. The immortality of the soul becomes necessary, in such a schema, because there is no way in which the goal could be reached without a life beyond the present temporal one.

In the climate of the German Enlightenment in which Kant lived, with its general disparagement of religious dogma and its respect for what it called reason and morality, his reliance on a moral law as the basis for the postulates of God, freedom and immortality, was certainly impressive. His argument on this subject deeply affected all important European and American thought for more than a century. Though he remains for other reasons of crucial importance in the history of ideas, comparatively few people today are as impressed as were his contemporaries in his moral argument for the three postulates. That is because his basic premise, the existence of a cosmic moral law corresponding to the laws of physics, would by no means enjoy the wide support today that it did in his time and for long continued to enjoy after his death.

Reincarnationist views, as they have been developed in Hinduism and Buddhism, rely for their appeal on the underlying doctrine of karma. Karmic doctrine *is* a statement of the existence of just such a law as Kant formulates as the basis of his three postulates. Its defenders, like Kant, presuppose a moral law that is to them obvious and apart from which speculations about God and human freedom and an afterlife would be unconvincing conjectures. It is karma that gives intelligibility and persuasiveness to the metaphysical notions that Hindu and Buddhist thought have inherited from their common upanishadic tradition. One would expect, therefore, that Kant, so far as he knew about such karmic notions, should have found himself sympathetic to them, to say the least. An investigation into his attitude produces somewhat ambiguous results; but we should consider them carefully in view of the importance of the link between Kant's presuppositions in his *Critique of Practical Reason* and those underlying the oriental notion of karma.

We must note first of all that Europeans in the eighteenth century knew very little about oriental thought and what they did know was usually very confused in their minds. Even thinkers of the stature of David Hume and Dugald Stewart, when they talk of "the Hindoos", show that they have little understanding of Indian thought and make far-fetched generalizations about it. Serious work in oriental studies, though it had begun, was still in its infancy in Europe and did not really get under way till far into the nineteenth century. We must not expect, therefore, that Kant should be well-informed on the subject from a modern standpoint. Nevertheless, we do find that in his early years he engaged in some remarkable speculations. In 1755, two centuries before space travel was to be taken seriously as a scientific and technological

possibility, Kant wrote a paper in which he indulged in an ad-
mittedly wild speculation that human souls might be destined to
start their pilgrimage from the planet nearest the sun and then
pursue it, planet by planet, to the extremities of our solar system.
Referring to what he called "the endless duration of the immortal
soul throughout the infinity of time," he suggests that it would be
parochial to suppose that the soul spends all its pilgrimage on
earth. Is it not more reasonable to suppose that it goes to "those far
distant globes of the cosmic system" that "already provoke our
curiosity"? He even toys with the notion that some distant planets
may be "in a state of preparation as a new dwelling place for us to
occupy after we have completed the period of time allotted for our
sojourn here." One day, perhaps, he suggests, we may be on the
planet Jupiter, for instance, and illumined by its satellites.[1]

In his maturer work, Kant dissociates himself from what he
specifically calls "fantastical theosophic dreams." What he seems
to be attacking, however, is not the karmic principle but, rather,
neo-Gnostic metaphysical chemistries that he knew to be fashionable in certain circles in eighteenth century Germany. Arguing that
the moral law is of such an inexorable nature that it necessitates the
realization of its object, the *summum bonum,* he goes on to show
the entailment of endless moral progress, which in turn entails the
existence and personality of the individual rational being. Without
the principle of such a moral destination, we fall into one or other
of two traps. Either we degrade the notion of the moral law,
looking upon it as something conformable to our convenience and
inclination, or else we arrogantly and irresponsibly indulge in
visions of grandeur in which we can pretend to the attainment of
moral perfection without a working out of the moral law.[2] Kant
apparently had in mind here the pretense, an ever-present danger
in Gnostic systems such as those with which he would have been
familiar, that the initiate, by reason of his knowledge of the mysteries of the universe, can be quickly deified. Moral evolution
becomes unnecessary. The initiate thinks himself above the law.

That is, of course, a danger in almost all forms of religion. It is a
notorious danger, for instance, in Christianity, in which it gave rise
to the term "antinomian" for those who feel that, since God is on
their side and has elected them to salvation, they cannot do wrong.
Some Muslims similarly defend everything that Muhammad did on
the ground that, since he was the special prophet of Allah, whatever he did must have been right, whether it seems so or not to our

moral sensibilities. Gnostic forms of religion are not alone in their susceptibility to such dangers, which spring from the arrogance that is part of our human nature. So strikingly similar, not least from our modern perspective, are the presuppositions common to karmic doctrine in the East and Kant's teaching in the West that the concept of karma could not but have appealed to him in principle, had he known and properly understood it, even if it would not necessarily have led him to reincarnationist views.

Whatever we think of reincarnationism, the notion that we reap what we sow appeals to all who believe, for one reason or another, that there is a moral principle or agent at the core of the universe. Once that is granted, something such as Kant's postulates follows, though not necessarily in precisely the way he formulated it. Certainly the freedom of the human will follows, at least to the extent that I must have the capacity to do what I know I ought to do. If I ought, I can. If, moreover, I am to be able to fulfil all my rightful moral ambitions and attain the realization of my moral ideals, I must have a life beyond the present one. What sort of life might it be? Kant himself, we have seen, toyed in his youth with the notion that it might be life on another planet. What we know today about the mind-body problem poses insuperable difficulties in the way of any proposal that the afterlife might be in a disembodied state. In any case, orthodox Christians would find such a notion quite contrary to the biblical promise of resurrection. Moral growth and development, such as we have seen to be a very plausible interpretation of the Christian doctrine of purgatory or the "intermediate state", seem to call for an afterlife involving something very like a reincarnationist understanding of it. For such a *saṁsāra*, such a series of rebirths, provides just the opportunity for further moral evolution that our moral consciousness, if we have anything like a Kantian one, seems to imply.

In the history of religions, the myth of reincarnation is most characteristically presented as a resolution of the problem of karmic guilt. As Dr. Vycinas puts it in a Heideggerian study, "the karmic debt is resolved by man's next incarnation or by his next life. Man is born to restore the harmony with the 'paradise lost.' "[3] Professor Eliade alludes frequently to this notion of a golden age in the "past" which is really a timelessness, an *illud tempus* that is non-temporal.[4] Karma is a burden on man, and it is that burden that leads him to the search for deliverance. "What shall I do to be saved?" No resolution is ever final, however. A new birth is sought in an attempt to restore the balance man has lost and so eradicate the guilt; but the pendulum that had swung too much in one direction now swings too much in another, and so it goes on. The wheel of rebirth never stops except by the abandonment of life itself. While it is true that nirvana has been often misunderstood by occidentals as a mere flowing of the individual rivers and streams into an ocean in which they are lost, it is certainly very unlike any recognizably Christian notion of heaven. Indeed, the notion of individuality is comparatively modern. Even Plato, from whom the West draws so much inspiration, underestimated it, to say the least: that is why his ideal State looks alarmingly totalitarian to even the most sympathetic modern reader. Within any schema that takes individuality seriously, karma can have no end, for it is a law of being. What I am to propose is that, while it may indeed be such a law of being, it may not be the whole law of being. In no other way could reincarnationism be christened.

The history of the faith-and-works controversy in Christian thought is a special one. There are, indeed, counterparts in other religions, notably in Buddhism. There too, reliance on faith can degenerate in ways comparable to the antinomianism into which, as has just been noted, Christianity can fall. In Tibetan Buddhism, sometimes called Vajrayana (contradistinguished from Hinayana and Mahayana), reliance on the name of Buddha found expression in the use of prayer-wheels, some of which have had little paddles attached to them so that they could be turned automatically when the blades were dipped into a stream and so continue to work for months or even years on end. I have seen mechanical rosaries advertized in American magazines, for use in automobiles, which is surely a close runner-up to the magic of the prayer-wheel. The classic Buddhist outlook, however, is one in which salvation is by works. One lifetime is by no means enough for working out one's salvation, so reincarnationism within the law of karma fits well into the basic concept of the way in which salvation is attainable. In Christianity, despite Paul's strong emphasis in the other direction, the situation has always been more ambiguous.

Certainly for Paul the uniqueness and great joy of the Christian faith lies in the discovery that "what makes a man righteous is not obedience to the Law, but faith in Jesus Christ."[5] This was a theologically subtle point in Paul's teaching, and not all among his contemporaries appreciated it. James, for instance, and Clement of Rome, seem to think more in terms of salvation by works.

Augustine, however, drawing from his own personal experience of divine grace, which he felt was entirely unmerited, championed the view that without grace moral improvement is impossible. Grace is the primary condition of salvation, and it is initiated by God. The Christian responds to it in faith. In the early Middle Ages, Augustine's view became the official view of the Roman Church; nevertheless, in practice, ordinary people in the Middle Ages in the West had a strong tendency to think in terms of works as the way to salvation. Hence the emphasis on various exercises such as the recitation of certain prayers, the making of barefoot pilgrimages, visiting churches or (in the case of those financially capable) building them. Luther, an Augustinian friar, was led through his reading of Paul's letters to an appreciation of the Pauline and Augustinian emphasis on grace to engage in the Reformation, a movement that tragically divided Western Christendom. The whole question of the relation of grace and works to each other in the process of salvation has always been and has remained complex. If a notion such as karma were to be acclimated to Christianity, it would have to be fitted into a very intricate framework.

For the karmic principle that makes reincarnationist doctrine morally acceptable is plainly a salvation-by-works principle. I alone am responsible for my condition. I alone can redeem myself from it. True, I may be helped in certain ways by a spiritual master or guru; but the help is only the kind of help that a good French teacher can give me when I am struggling to master that language. He can train me to speak well; he can encourage me to learn the vocabularies; he can drill me in the grammar; but in the last resort it is I who must learn French. No one else can do it for me. The role of the teacher is by no means the role of a savior. He is no more a savior than a midwife is a mother. In the Pauline-Augustinian interpretation of Christianity is an emphasis on a debt we owe to God that is far beyond and qualitatively unlike any debt we could ever owe to a teacher or guru. The karmic principle would appear to be, therefore, a repudiation of all that is most distinctive in the Christian Way.

That, however, is only one side of the issue, important though it be. For as Paul and Augustine and Luther all knew, each in his own way, grace is not a gift that comes packaged like a birthday present. It is a fundamental healing that makes possible our spiritual advancement. Without it we can do nothing; with it we can and we must. We do what we are called to do. To put grace in a drawer like a birthday gift would be to repudiate it. So of course works play a great part in the process of salvation. Without works the faith that should be our response to grace is not only dead,[6] it becomes a corpse that is an impediment to our growth. There is a strong Christian witness, exemplified today very strikingly in the thought of Dietrich Bonhoeffer, as well as in various forms of Christian existentialism, that, whatever a Christian believes about God and divine grace, he or she must live as if there were no God and therefore no divine grace on which to rely. To take this attitude in practice, as opposed to theological theory, is what it means to begin the process of growing up. No doubt, from a Christian standpoint, grace is a pre-condition of moral evolution; but the moral evolution takes place only when we stand on our own feet. Doing so does not diminish a genuine Christian's gratitude for the ability to do it. One must not, however, confuse the ability with the act. Therein, precisely, lies the antinomian heresy. The antinomian sits down while saying "Hooray, by the grace of God, I can stand on my own two feet." Christian gratitude is properly expressed, rather, in the act of standing up more and more effectively on one's own two feet without ever forgetting how one came by the capacity to do so.

What we have seen of the concept of purgatory suggests that there is no fundamental reason why the whole *saṁsāra* or reincarnational chain should not be a series of purgatorial steps. This life might be to my last life as the fifth grade is to the fourth, and to my next life as the fifth is to the sixth. As karmic doctrine is generally presented, graduation (be it conceived as nirvana or in some other way) is an inevitable ending to the process. Moral evolution may take a long time or a short: my follies may delay it, my heroisms accelerate it. There is no reason, however, why we must acquiesce in that interpretation. We might well say, rather: "The process is interminable, because no sooner do I achieve growth in one direction than I atrophy in another. As in playing the violin, most people can learn up to a point; but then they level off and in the end they stick, unable to master the instruments. As the Bible has it, many are called but few are chosen." Then we could see the *saṁsāra* as both a state of growth, development, and purgation, on the one hand, and, on the other, that from which we need to be saved. Or to put the situation another way, as Paul told the Galatians they had been slaves under the Law but now through

Christ are made sons and heirs,[7] so through the grace of God in Christ the Christian might be so emancipated as to succeed in the moral evolution provided by the *saṃsāra* under the karmic law, where before he saw no way of success. There is an infinite difference between a purgatory that leads nowhere and one that is in fact a purification, a growth, and a development leading to final fulfilment. The former kind of purgatory would then take on all the characteristics of hell, and according to tradition that is precisely what Christians are supposed to be saved from.

Superficially, there would seem to be a counterpart to this very notion. For in Hindu lore there is, besides *karma-yoga,* the way of salvation by works, another way, *bhakti-yoga,* salvation by faith. There is, however, no real analogy between that schema and the one I am suggesting as a possibility. Hinduism and its Buddhist offshoots love to speak of alternative roads, all of which lead to the same destination. If Christianity is worth talking about it all, it provides something very different indeed from any such alternative opening in the forest. It claims to provide egress, where other roads lead endlessly through a maze. Yet the egress is not an easy escape. God does not promise to cause me to grow without my growing. He promises only the conditions for success. If you had been growing unsuccessfully for a trillion incarnations, that would be very good news. Not all are ready for it, for not all have yet discovered the futility of moral evolution by karma, as not all were ready to see with Paul that the Law of Moses, while it shows one what one should do, does not help one to do it.[8]

REFERENCES AND NOTES

[1]*Allgemeine Naturgeschichte und Theorie des Himmels* (Koenigsberg and Leipzig: 1755), p. 198.

[2]T. K. Abbot, tr., *Critique of Practical Reason,* 4th revised ed. (London: Longmans, Green and Company, 1889), p. 218.

[3]Vincent Vycinas, *Search for Gods* (The Hague: Martinus Nijhoff, 1972), p. 262.

[4]E.g., M. Eliade, *Myths, Dreams, and Mysteries* (New York: Harper Torchbooks, 1967), Chapter III ("Nostalgia for Paradise in the Primitive Traditions"), p. 59. *See also* p. 49.

[5]Galatians 2.16 (J.B.).

[6]James 2. 17, 20, 26.

[7]Galatians 4.1-11.

[8]Romans 7.19.

XII

SALVATION, PROVIDENCE AND GRACE

Grace does not destroy nature
but perfects it.

Thomas Aquinas

In light of the ambiguities we have seen in the Christian doctrine of the afterlife, we must raise anew the old question: from what precisely is the Christian supposed to be saved? When Dr. Johnson once expressed the fear that he might be damned, he was asked by his host, Dr. Adams: "What do you mean by 'damned'?" To this Dr. Johnson replied ("passionately and loudly," according to his biographer): "Sent to hell, Sir, and punished everlastingly."[1] While I would be less dramatic than the celebrated lexicographer, I am inclined to the view that we are saved from a fate that some of us would account even more terrifying: extinction.

Paul certainly taught that "the wage paid by sin is death."[2] The unredeemed, therefore, die. That is the end of them. The good news is that, since Jesus Christ has risen, we also are raised from death to eternal life. "When this perishable nature has put on imperishability, and when this mortal nature has put on immortality, then the words of scripture will come true: *Death is swallowed up in victory. Death, where is your victory? Death, where is your sting?*"[3] Clearly, according to Paul, annihilation by death is the

117

only expectation the unredeemed may entertain. In fact, moreover, to judge from the conversation and attitudes of those who do not account themselves redeemed by Jesus Christ, death is the only expectation they do entertain. The arrangement that Paul envisions seems admirable: both the redeemed and the unredeemed get what they expect. We might well add the suggestion that each receives what he or she is capable of receiving. To such an arrangement not even the most stiffnecked of moralizers could well object.

Two questions immediately arise: (a) what are the merits of such a proposal? and (b) what precisely does it entail for a Christian scheme of salvation?

Paul's teaching on this subject appears to many a mere mollification of what they take to be the more generally accepted Christian doctrine of heaven and hell as the only two possible final destinations of humankind. It is by no means merely that. The notion that the unredeemed should be simply annihilated expresses in the most horrific way the plight of humanity apart from redemption through Jesus Christ. Those who, bound and blinded by their sinful state, have no hope of a personal afterlife do indeed rightly assess their own worth. They are rightly like "pig's meat priced," for they can neither want nor claim to be more than tragically specialized and highly organized mammals. The question of an afterlife simply does not arise. By contrast, the capacity for everlasting life and its attainment through association with the resurrection of Christ gives rise to a joy beyond all anyone could ask or think. The difference between the two conditions, annihilation by death and resurrection to life everlasting, is infinite.

Were the situation so simple, the contrast would be indeed fearsome to contemplate. But dare one take all those who are not radiant sheep to be all cloddish goats? What of the millions who do cherish hope of personal survival yet could not possibly be accounted saved by Christ? "This Good News of the kingdom," we are told, "will be proclaimed to the whole world as a witness to all the nations. And then the end will come."[4] True, the Evangelist no doubt has in mind the fall of Jerusalem, which occurred in A.D. 70, and when he writes of "the world" he can be thinking only, of course, of the world as known to the people of the Near East and Mediterranean lands; nevertheless, a problem is raised that our knowledge of the contemporary world only makes more acute. Millions of Hindus, Jews, Muslims, and others cannot be written off as bereft of all sense of personal immortality; yet they certainly cannot be classed among those who have been partakers of everlasting life through association with the resurrection of Jesus Christ. Are we to suppose them to have been annihilated for ever, despite their longing for and belief in an afterlife? Surely not. To believe at all in an afterlife is surely to testify to the beginning, at least, of the saving action of God and of their affirmative response to it. That they should be doomed to extinction is as intolerable in its way as is the notion of unbaptized infants crawling on the floor of hell. Plausible indeed, then, would be the notion that they are already at a stage of their pilgrimage but, unable to complete it within the compass of this present life, will be accorded further lives, affording them further opportunities to grasp and respond to the Good News that is addressed to all who long for everlasting life.

Is such a notion compatible with the Pauline doctrine of conditional immortality, that is, immortality that is dependent on one's being "raised up" to victory over death through the resurrection of Christ? In view of the infinite gulf between the sheep and the goats that is entailed in Paul's teaching, not only does the notion seem compatible; its absence would make Paul's teaching positively disgusting. Here is a precocious little Quaker girl who has developed a strong sense of personal identity and deep longing for personal survival yet has not happened to hear of the resurrection of Christ. No one at meeting mentioned it, or, if someone did, she did not grasp its meaning for human salvation. In this state of ignorance she is killed in a street accident and, birthright Quaker that she is, dies unbaptized. Is she to be written off in the same category as a smug materialistic oaf who has never seriously entertained a thought about God, freedom, or immortality, in the course of his long life? Or take this little boy, a budding Bhakti saint, who is carried off in an epidemic in Calcutta: is he, too, destined for no better a fate than was deserved by a Nero or a Hitler? Roman Catholic theologians, in an attempt to mitigate the horror of the traditional doctrine of hell, frequently resort to the use of the term "invincible ignorance" to provide such innocent people with an excuse for their failure to accept the teachings of the Church. Surely, however, they need more than an excuse. They need and deserve further opportunity. Otherwise the scheme of salvation must appear not merely arbitrary but ludicrously mechanical. That Hitler and the little Quaker girl should be treated exactly alike is what we have come to expect from computers. The tendency so to treat people is built into democratic societies, in which everybody is a quantitative unit like so many pills in a box. Societies that are run like that may perform certain political and social functions efficiently; but mercifully they are not charged with the arrangements for our final destiny. The Kingdom of God is no such society. If it were, it would be a cosmic monster, alien to everything that Christians take God to be.

The lame-duck doctrine of invincible ignorance does, however, perform service of a kind. It calls to our attention the unsatisfactoriness of the whole structure of our eschatology. One cannot have Hitler and the little Quaker girl walking down the steps of hell together. So the little girl gets a free pass-out check to take her to some pleasanter abode. But that will not do, because she is not yet ready to use it. She does not know the way and cannot read the directions. What she needs is a chance to develop and mature. If God is what Christians take him to be, he denies no one such opportunity.

The notion that extinction or annihilation is the fate from which we can be saved through the power of Jesus Christ sits well with all that we know of the evolutionary nature of all created beings. Entropy does occur. There is a waste product in the evolutionary process. That is what the whole conception of Gehenna really means. As the dinosaur died out after something like twenty million years, so individuals at our highly organized level of being and consciousness may simply extinguish themselves. Presumably, however, one does not reach this high level of awareness that is associated with all that is traditionally called "human" without hope of eventual victory. As in the parable of the sower, many seeds come to naught; yet by the time we reach the human level of consciousness we should expect many chances for growth and development before we either become fit for nothing but the trash bin or achieve the victory that assures everlasting life. A reincarnational view provides just such opportunities, without necessarily excluding extreme cases in which the individual has either rendered himself incapable of survival beyond this present life or has achieved such extraordinary capabilities that he or she is ready for more than any life within the human condition can offer.

All this is especially compatible with the Christian emphasis on resurrection, as developed in Paul's teaching. Here there is no question of immortality of the soul, as in traditional Hindu doctrines and as in Plato's view of the soul as an essentially immortal "substance". As we saw in an earlier chapter, the doctrine of hell, with its attendant horrors, is intended as a logical development of the notion that, since man is intrinsically immortal and some men turn out badly, they cannot enjoy the presence of God. Having permanently deprived themselves of the capacity to enjoy that presence, they must for ever endure the sense of its loss, the *poena damni,* as the medieval theologians called it. The premise with which such reasoning begins is false: the notion that we are intrinsically immortal has no foundation in the biblical teaching that is at the root of Christian faith. The notion of hell also functions, however, as a symbol for the loss of being, while that of heaven symbolizes, of course, the opposite, the fullness of being. Professor Macquarrie expresses doubt that "anyone ever comes to the point of utterly losing his personal being, or of falling away altogether from the potentialities of such being."[5] He will not commit himself to a doctrine of conditional immortality. Yet he sees that the "utter limit of hell would be annihilation of the possibility of personal being. Since salvation itself is personal, and must therefore be freely accepted, God cannot impose it upon anyone, so we must at least leave open the possibility that this kind of annihilation might be the final destiny for some."[6] In the end, however, he balks at the idea, on the ground that there can be no "sharp line between the 'righteous' and the 'wicked'."[7] The very considerations that have for long led me to conclude to a doctrine of conditional immortality seem to lead him away from it.[8] How should this be?

Professor Macquarrie is disinclined to envision extremes in the range of finite being. He neither sees heaven as necessarily the final plenitude and total realization of being nor hell as its total loss. For him hell is the crippling of being and heaven an eminent degree of its joy. In all this I much sympathize with Macquarrie's outlook. I think, however, that he reacts too strongly against the Scottish Calvinism in which he was nurtured. He is chary of the high stance taken by the Augustinianism that lies behind Calvin's thought. Here also I am not without sympathy; yet I am more impressed than he seems to be by the fundamental indisposition of so many people toward the notion of personal survival. I find that a very large number of people simply do not entertain it at all and many do not find the notion even congenial. They do not even want to be "raised up" to new life. They readily accept Santayana's notion that life is somewhat like a dance to which the dancers go in the evening, full of energy and wishing it could go on for ever but from which they quite happily depart in the early hours of the morning, being weary and feeling the time has come for the ball to finish. At best they say of life: "Let someone else take up where I left off. I have begotten some children. I have some accomplishments to my credit. Now I want to take my ease for a few years and then 'pass away', preferably, of course, without discomfort." I find, moreover, that this is by no means an attitude confined to people who have rejected or turned away from Christian faith. On not a few occasions I have discovered it quite clearly and openly expressed by church people who are apparently quite active in parish work. An elderly Episcopalian couple, both of outstandingly sterling character and admirable reliability who played active roles in their prominent parish for many years, recently told me, in answer to my inquiry, that they felt quite sure that death would bring them final extinction. They seemed very well pleased by the prospect. What they had been thinking of all these years as they proclaimed the words of the Creed and received, at the altar, assurances of everlasting life, is beside the point. The point is that they are quite typical of vast numbers of people, including a great many churchmen and churchwomen. Sad though it be that such is the case, I cannot make sense of the notion that they might have everlasting life thrust upon them, contrary to their wishes. They have lived good lives according to their own standards, using the Church as an arena for doing some charitable works but paying no particular attention to what the Bible and the Church actually say, presumably taking it to be part of the furnishings that give churches their antique charm. Surely the inevitable conclusion must be that they are among those of whom Jesus says "they have had their reward.⁹ They ask for no more. How could they receive more?

Others who have barely heard of the Church's teachings yearn for some sort of return to earth, another chance to do and learn more. That seems to me to augur far better for their eventually taking hold of everlasting life. They are among those who "want to be saved," that is, saved from what Macquarrie calls "the utter limit of hell," annihilation. In another life the disclosure may come to them; the divine penny may drop into the chink they have left open. Reincarnationism provides limitless opportunities for all who are able to take them. I think, however, that, if we are to believe in the possibility of an afterlife at all, we must face the possibility of spiritual entropy: at least in some cases annihilation is inevitable. As I take reincarnation to be the vehicle of purgatory, I take annihilation to be what hell really means, and truly terrible is that fate. We had best defer for the present what is to be understood by heaven. That vision belongs to our last chapter.

Evidence was produced earlier in this study sufficient to explode the widespread notion that there is some historical reason why reincarnation cannot be christened. One might well ask, however, whether there may not be an even more radical, theological objection. The late Dr. A. C. Ewing, in a sympathetic but critical treatment, raises it aptly.[10] This Cambridge philosopher asks whether there is not a "mercantile flavour about the conception" of "an exact proportion between such incommensurables as goodness and happiness," such as is envisioned in the karmic law that what you sow you will reap. He points out that a universe in which there was an exact proportion between goodness and happiness and between badness and unhappiness would be one in which there could be no genuine self-sacrifice.

Ewing's point is well-taken. It touches, moreover, all that is nearest the heart of the Christian. With a moral calculus such as is written into the law of karma, how could there be any place for the love and compassion, the self-humbling and the self-abnegation, that are so fundamental to the Christian life? If God is of such a nature that he would give himself in Christ to be crucified "for us men and for our salvation,' and if he is indeed "the lamb slain from the foundation of the world,"[11] how can a doctrine such as reincarnation, which depends on the law of the karma, be christened? Is it not like baptizing a company's balance sheet or profit and loss account? Everything we are told of Christ, everything that leads the Christian to accept Christ as his or her Savior, tells of a generosity so immense, of a love so selfless, that it has no conceivable place for any such mathematical reckoning. Typical of the Christian's conversion experience is the awareness that if God were looking for merit he would certainly look elsewhere. He saved "even me" is the cry of every Christian who knows how unworthy he is to be, in C. S. Lewis's felicitous phrase "surprised by joy," the recipient of the "amazing grace" that has no relation at all to any moral calculus. I am saved, not through a trillion rebirths but, as Augustine says, *inter pontem et fontem* or, in William Camden's well-known lines:

> *Betwixt the stirrup and the ground*
> *Mercy I asked, mercy I found.*

Christian love knows nothing of calculations: it is prodigal. Like the widow in the Gospel who threw in all she had, God so loves the world that he gives his all. He does not employ a cost accountant to advise him whether the operation is fiscally sound. He humbles himself to the point of encamping with needy humanity, even to the point of being crucified for it. Apart from that, Christianity has no message. It is to Good Friday that the Christian looks to see the kind of love that makes the cosmos tick:

> *O dearly, dearly has He loved,*
> *And we must love Him too,*
> *And trust in His redeeming blood,*
> *And try His works to do.*

To talk to a Christian about karma would seem to be somewhat like talking of the cost of living to a girl in love: what could be more irrelevant? There is a strain of madness in all love, and it is precisely that "foolishness" (as Paul called it) that makes the Christian want to give to the uttermost in response to the stupendous magnanimity of the love of God. We may recall how Origen's mother, in her prudence, had to hide Origen's clothes, to restrain him from rushing forth to invite martyrdom. Whatever a Christian may or may not be, he cannot be one who counts the cost. How, then, could he entertain any system of moral accountancy such as the karmic law entails?

Considerations of that kind weigh heavily so long as the typical Hindu and Buddhist presentation of karma as a scheme of salvation is taken to be an alternative to the Christian one. When, however, we think of karma as standing in the same relation to the Christian Way that the Mosaic Law stands to the Gospel, the objection seems to lose most, if not all, of its force. The self-emptyingness of God to which the Christian is called to respond becomes, then, the way of salvation that frees us from the imprisoning aspect of the karmic law and enables us to use it, rather, as a springboard for release. Instead of the sense of weariness one might well feel at the prospect of submission to the karmic principle for countless rebirths to come, the Christian could see in it (as, in traditional Catholic doctrine, does the soul entering purgatory) a cause for rejoicing, knowing as he does that he is on the way to eternal bliss and everlasting life. As a matter of fact, certain forms of Mahayana Buddhism do say something suggestive of that, in their own religious idiom: the return of the bodhisattvas to aid humankind. We need not concern ourselves here with how Mahayana came to develop that notion, or under what influence it did so. The point is that karma can be both a fetter and an instrument of escape. There seems no good reason, then, why the Christian scheme of salvation should not encompass karma and rebirth as the Gospel encompasses and completes the Law.

If, then, reincarnationism may be acclimated to the Christian soteriological scheme, what role might be played by the Christian doctrines of providence and grace? Would not they be in some way attenuated? Let us look first at the doctrine of providence.

That God provides and cares for his creatures is, of course, a fundamental tenet of Christian faith, rooted in the Bible. The question is: how does he do it? "Who makes provision for the raven when his squabs cry out to God and crane their necks in hunger?" (Job 38.41) asked Job, inspired by God, to answer his chiding friends in the midst of his suffering. Trust that God will provide what is needed by the creature is never doubted in the Bible; but the Bible is no less unequivocal in teaching that what he provides may be a very bitter pill. We tend to think of providence as coming to the rescue with a cushion when the going gets rough; but, on the contrary, God seems often to provide a goad rather than a cushion, and no less often a mist that obscures his presence and sorely tries the pilgrim's hope and trust. Providence does not always smile; more often it frowns, though hid behind the frown God be smiling in love, as William Cowper suggests:

> Behind a frowning providence
> He hides a smiling face.

Such is Christian faith in the goodness of God, the love that is at the core of all things. The superficially religious tend to expect that, while Nature is indifferent if not hostile to us, God is to be expected to leap through Nature, so to speak, and come to the aid of the wounded pilgrim. After all, is not that precisely what he is believed to have done in the Incarnation that is the focus of all Christian faith? Does not God in his providence somehow suspend Nature?

Of course not. God no more suspends Nature than he suspends history. Christian teaching is that he suspends neither but transforms both. He transforms Nature by investing his children with the self-abnegating power to overcome it; he transforms history by introducing into it the new dimension that can be experienced by those who see him as delivering them from history's inexorable power. In short, through Christ, God sacramentalizes Nature and history. When we speak, then, of his providence, we are speaking of the goodness of God in working all things out for our good, whatever be the means that are necessary for that end.

Nevertheless, the Christian can also rightfully believe that God can and does point out to us doors that we did not notice were open. He can and does tell us what the tools in our kit are for. That is, indeed, the proper end of prayer: not to take away opportunity from us and substitute for it a cozy and relaxing pillow, but to help us to see how we must and can help ourselves, if we are to grow, as grow we must, to our full stature. The mystery of evil remains in Christian as in all other forms of religious belief; but when we inspect the nature of its challenge to Christian faith we find that the absence of a doctrine of rebirth injects a peculiar and unnecessary puzzle into the notoriously thorny problem. No one need boggle at the notion of an agony that results in development, growth, and a new dimension of life, as happens in childbirth when the pain of child-bearing ends in the radiant joy of motherhood and new life. But what if it ends in the birth of a moron or of a paralytic? No one, looking back on his own life, is likely to doubt God's love and care when he has seen years of poverty or disease overcome. Doubts arise when, as so often happens, one's labors seem to progress well and one's prayers seem to be favorably received, till suddenly all comes toppling down in utter chaos as if to mock one for the sliver of meaning one had succeeded in extracting for a while from one's life.

Death is the supreme instance of such tragedy, because it intrudes with such incoherence and irrelevance into whatever rationality one has been able to find in life. The little child does well at school, grows apparently strong and vigorous in body and mind, shows signs of developing into a sweet and compassionate human being, then suddenly is pronounced a victim of leukemia and under sentence of imminent death. That a cure may be round the corner in medical research only aggravates the anguish of the parents and others who note that it is too late to help their beloved child. Or a man is taken just as he is on the verge of accomplishing the task for which he is uniquely fitted, a task that perhaps no other can do as he would have done it. Such tragedies are tragic because we think we have but one little life to live, and they stand out against what we see in the lives of others who escape such extreme anguish. The Christian assurance that death is not the end does not *in itself* diminish the problem, for though we sigh that the wicked seem to prosper while the righteous suffer, not *all* the righteous suffer so cruelly as do some, nor, indeed, do the wicked all prosper according to their wickedness. The end of human life is peculiarly inconclusive in so many ways, and when Christians are told that after death the future is bright and their cross will be exchanged for a crown, the assurance does nothing to explain why Bob's cross should be so much more terrible than Bill's.

By introducing the notion of reincarnation into the providential scheme, the absurdity in the problem of evil is immeasurably mitigated. Moreover, as soon as it is introduced, one may well wonder why it was not introduced before. The answer *may be* that the doctrine, not uncommonly held in the primitive Christian Church, was artificially and more or less accidentally inhibited through a great misunderstanding. If so, it would not be for the first time that Christians would have had to acknowledge that in the history of Christian thought one old way of looking at things had come to be exchanged for another newer, fuller and more satisfying understanding of the eternal truths revealed by God in his Word. The new dimension that evolutionary thinking brought to Christian faith a hundred years ago is an example that springs readily to mind. Few people in the ancient Church and throughout the centuries could have guessed at such a way of interpreting the Creation. A literalistic understanding of Genesis was for long very widespread. Certainly the belief in the separate creation of the various zoological species, and acceptance of them as not related to one another in any evolutionary way, was a virtually universal assumption for many centuries. Only toward the end of the nineteenth century did religious people (and even then only, at first, very deeply religious people) come to see that an evolutionary understanding of biology could shed new light on and immeasurably enchance a Christian's faith in God as Creator. It enabled one to make more sense of a traditional doctrine. Might not reincarnationism be in the same case?

We fret over the mystery of pain and suffering, the whole problem of evil as philosophers have come to call it; but it is not really the pain or the suffering that troubles the Christian, for to these he has become accustomed in living the Christian life, and above all in knowing the cost of redemption: the Cross. What is so puzzling to even the men and women whose faith is deepest and most firmly established is the astounding absurdity they see on every hand. Reincarnationist belief does not remove the pain or the suffering from our vision of human destiny; but it does much to take away the absurdity, the tragic disproportionateness that sits so ill with all the rest of our Christian experience. The absurdity recedes when this life is seen, not as a brief flash of time in which decisions for all eternity are made, but as a chapter in, or slice of, an immensely longer evolutionary process, the process of making us what we are meant to be, the process of realizing our full moral and spiritual potential by every means available within the infinitely merciful providence of God. If we were to accept reincarnationism into Christian belief, God's ways would still be mysterious; but they might better reveal the will of God to us who walk in faith. If the now traditional absence of reincarnationism from the Christian vision of human destiny should have been a merely artificial obstacle, as may be suspected, its restoration would enable us to take possession of our faith in greater plenitude.

What we have been saying emerges from seeing our question in relation to the vital importance of the freedom and responsibility that are too often neglected in our understanding of divine providence. There is, however, a correlative Christian doctrine, apart from which Christian faith would be meaningless: the doctrine of grace. Man, endowed with free will, the exercise of which is essential to his moral growth, cannot ever begin to grow without God's aid. Grace, which bestows that aid, is to human freedom somewhat as is capital to labor in economics. Perhaps that is why its relation to free will has produced the bitterest and longest theological controversy in the history of the Christian Church. Christians have never been in any doubt of the need for divine grace. The controversies have been about the mode of its operation. Tertullian was probably the first of the Christian Fathers to attempt to formulate it. He accounted grace the divine energy at work in the human soul. Augustine, two centuries later, developed a much more elaborate exposition of the theology of grace, in the course of his controversy with Pelagius, and as a result of that controversy. Thomas Aquinas, nine centuries later still, adhered in principle to Augustine's teaching on this subject, though he further developed it; but the debate was renewed with zeal in the

Reformation and Counter-Reformation controversies and was the central issue in the disputes between the Jansenists and their opponents in seventeenth century France.

Now, we have seen that the karmic principle implies moral freedom and responsibility. According to reincarnationist belief, I alone am responsible for my karma. I have no one else to blame or to praise for it. I alone have woven it and I am even now weaving for myself the karma that is to be mine in my next life. We may well say, therefore, that in reincarnationism there are no cosmic free lunches. The reincarnationist, believing that nothing is to be expected from chance, has no room in his scheme either for cosmic gambling or for divine bequests. So he can say with Matthew Arnold:

> Yet they, believe me, who await
> No gifts from Chance, have conquered Fate.

In this attitude to chance and fate he is at one, of course, with Catholic and Evangelical Christians; but how could he ever say, in John Bradford's famous phrase, "There but for the grace of God go I," which is an expression of the sentiment of gratitude that is so much at the heart of Christian experience? The very notion of grace seems at first sight as foreign to karma as is kindness to chemistry.

Yet that may provide the very clue that we need to solve the central problem of the reconcilability of reincarnationism to the Christian faith. For, after all, surely nothing seemed more alien to the thought of the Jews, the people Christ chose as his own, than did the notion of the Incarnation of God in human flesh.[12] That notion seemed to strike at the very root of the whole biblical revelation of God's ways with man. It seemed to destroy the very concept of God as revealed in the Torah. Let us look more closely at grace with this suggestion in mind.

Grace is not a substitute for human goodness. It is, rather, the condition of its realization. Without God's grace I cannot even get off the ground; nor can I be sustained for one moment, at any stage of my development. My work, not least at its most arduous, depends on grace as its indispensable condition. If, as I have suggested, grace is to free will as capital is to labor, we can see how dependent we are upon it. It is that which makes possible the enterprise. Were I to sit back and spend the capital without investing it in the business, my business would be most certainly doomed at the outset. My creativity and my industry would go for naught. Yet capital without labor is fruitless. Jesus, according to the Gospel, was very hard on the man who failed to use the capital he had been given. (Matthew 23.14 ff.) To think of grace as interfering with human freedom is as foolish as would be the notion that capital interferes with labor; yet many have so misunderstood the nature of grace. The deep concern of Christians with "sin" is, of course, a concern about our helplessness apart from grace. To those who misunderstand the nature of grace, however, Christians seem to be moaning and groaning and beating their breasts about sin when they would be much better occupied getting up on their legs and doing something morally constructive. Indeed, from the point of view of this misunderstanding, "pardon, absolution and remission" of our sins is but a three-headed immorality. As Sir Oliver Lodge observed at the beginning of the present century: "the higher man of today is not worrying about his sins at all."[13] Many industrious men and women have likewise had their noses so deep in their work that they have never given much thought to what would happen if the capital behind it were to dry up.

If, then, we see grace as the fundamental condition of all the good we can do and all the moral and spiritual growth we can hope to attain, is there any basic reason why a system that is so essentially a work-ethic should not be illumined by the Christian doctrine of grace? Work-ethics have played a traditional role in the life and thought of the Christian Church. The New England Puritans provide only one example. More than a thousand years before the *Mayflower* sailed, the Benedictines had begun a monastic life that would have been meaningless apart from its emphasis on the dignity of labor: *orare est laborare,* to work is to pray, to pray is to work. Indeed, the very riches that were the inevitable fruit of that monastic tradition became eventually a snare to them. Why, then, should the karmic principle be accounted incompatible with the Christian doctrine of grace?

I cannot personally see any sound reason why reincarnationism should be accounted, either on historical or on theological grounds, irreconcilable with an orthodox Christian view of what God provides for the working out of the salvation that Christ, according to fundamental Christian belief, has made possible for those who can appropriate it. By that I do not mean to suggest that it should be promptly inserted into the articles of Christian faith. The Church has never been eager to formulate doctrines that must be believed, and it never should. It has generally insisted on such formulations only when forced into doing so. I do not pretend for a moment that reincarnationism is plainly taught in Scripture, even though we have seen some suggestions of it there. The fact that some, possibly a good many, Christians in the primitive Church believed in some form of reincarnation is interesting; but it is not a compelling reason for introducing it into the Christian creeds. Yet when all that is said, we can still say something that should startle many Christians. For if we have established, as I believe I have, that a form of reincarnationism is quite compatible with the central Christian tradition and not opposed to Scripture, then we have done much. For that means that Christians who find the notion helps them to make sense of their own faith, and who are not daunted by the philosophical and scientific objections we have considered, need have no qualms about accepting it as a viable option for an honest Christian. Far from diminishing the force of anything in Christian experience, it may vivify Christian faith, enrich Christian hope, deepen Christian love, and abundantly clarify the human mind. In our next chapter we shall consider how it might affect human relationships. The perspicacious reader will have seen already how it might affect the relation of Christianity to other religions.

REFERENCES AND NOTES

[1]James Boswell, *The Life of Samuel Johnson, LL.D.*, Vol. II (New York: Charles Scribner's Sons, n.d.), p. 647.

[2]Romans 6.23 (J.B.)

[3]I Corinthians 15:54f. Cf. Hosea 13.14.

[4]Matthew 24.14.

[5]John Macquarrie, *Principles of Christian Theology* (New York: Charles Scribner's Sons, 1966), p. 327.

[6]Ibid.

[7]Ibid.

[8]*See* my *Introduction to Religious Philosophy* (Boston: Houghton Mifflin, 1959), p. 208.

[9]Matthew 6.2, 5, 16. (J.B.)

[10]A. C. Ewing, "The Philosophy of McTaggart, with Special Reference to the Doctrine of Reincarnation". In *Aryan Path*, February, 1957.

[11]Revelation 13.8.

[12]In view of a recently popularized theological controversy, we should note that the

flat denial that Jesus is in any special way divine or the "full and final revelation" of God is one that has appeared periodically within Christian history. I take such a denial to be specifically and radically incompatible with Christian orthodoxy. Of course what precisely it *means* to say is that Jesus is fully divine and fully human (the Chalcedonian formula) is plainly an intricate theological question.

[13]O. Lodge, *Hibbert Journal*, 1904, p. 466.

XIII

CONSEQUENCES FOR MARRIAGE AND OTHER RELATIONSHIPS

Matches are made in heaven.
Robert Burton, *Anatomy of Melancholy*

The deep and enduring relationships that arise in lifelong friendship and *par excellence* in Christian marriage provide not only the best opportunities for outgrowing self-centeredness but the greatest possibilities of realizing the highest of earthly joys. In such relationships a father will give a kidney to save his child's life. Men and women will even lay down their lives, if need be, for those whom they most deeply love. So profound is the experience of such relationships that those who believe in any kind of afterlife naturally ask whether relationships that have meant so much to us are to be terminated by death as peremptorily as a business partnership. In plain English: shall we meet again?

Such is, of course, the fervent hope of many who have been deeply affected by personal relationships. So confused, however, is Christian eschatology that, apart from attempts in popular piety to celebrate the hope of union with loved ones in the life beyond, preachers are generally cautious when they treat the subject. They seem to be on the whole rather relieved when they do not have to treat it at all. The difficulties are, indeed, immense. Jesus, when asked about reunion in the afterlife, replied that men and women, when they rise from the dead, "do not marry; no, they are like the angels in heaven."[1] If the resurrection body is so different, how could we recognize one another at all, even if we could preserve our earthly memories? In any case, if memory is dependent on the brain, as all empirical studies indicate, how could I carry my memory with me to a life beyond after my brain had been destroyed by death? We have already seen in an earlier chapter how difficult is the notion of survival of the personality; but even if we overcome that difficulty we are faced with the even more intractable problem of memory. Yet in what could heaven consist if we were completely bereft of the memory of those very special relationships in which we learned how to love God, the eternal enjoyment of whom is, according to all the classical theologians, Catholic and Reformed, the very essence of heaven? True, I might presumably do mathematics after having completely forgotten my teacher, the school, the classrooms, the texts, that were an indispensable part of my acquiring my skill. But could I know the love of God after wholly forgetting the earthly relationships through which I was gradually brought to a knowledge of that love? Surely not. For loving God or man is not at all like doing mathematics. What would it mean to say I loved a person after memory of my whole relationship with that person had been *completely* obliterated? Gabriel Marcel, in his *Journal Métaphysique* raises, though in a very different way, the same kind of question.[2]

In fact, however we try to think of the possibility of deep love such as exists between a husband and wife who have been happily married for forty years, or friends who have been close to each other for such a length of time, we cannot get away from the presumption that some kind of memory is an implicate of the love. Of course much has been forgotten. Perhaps, if they are very old, the power of memory itself has begun to wane. The quality of the love certainly does not depend on the accuracy or spread of the memory; yet with the memory totally destroyed, the relationship would be literally dead. If death does destroy memory as completely as that, then taking up friendships and other human relationships in a life beyond is unintelligible, even if the possibility of an afterlife be conceded.

Suppose, however, that somewhere in the stream of energy we have called the soul could be hidden a vestige of memory such that it might be at least partially awakened in a future life. Suppose that, born into a new life, you continue for years oblivious of any previous existence and therefore, of course, any relationship prior to the life you are living. Then you meet a person who changes your self-awareness. You fall deeply in love with each other, so deeply that it does more than merely augur a happy marriage. Indeed, the marriage you seek seems unsuitable from every standpoint, psychological, social and economic. Yours is one of those unlikely happenings the romantics call romantic and the others dub unpropitious, if they are too polite to say disastrous. Not only are you socially and financially poles apart, so that you have a correspondingly different preparation for life and a different set of expectations; even apart from these barriers you seem temperamentally ill-matched. One partner is impulsive, quick-witted and quick-tempered, untidy, impatient, and outgoing, while the other is prudent, slow, tidy, and introspective. Your tastes differ no less than your education and temper. One of you is distinctly musical, the other almost tone-deaf. One is an avid reader, the other thumbs through magazines. Yet you both know you are right for each other. Even your quarrels cement your love. You are not only lovers; you are soul-mates.

Now suppose that you had really met and loved in a former life, perhaps through the course of a long marriage or friendship. The death of your partner or friend had been the most terrible blow you had ever sustained. Though you had recovered from it, you knew that two-thirds of you had died. The inimitable voice you loved was silent. Never again would you see the familiar face, the gentle hands, the hurrying feet that were a very part of yourself, of your face, your hands, your feet. Bravely you went on living; but it could only be, you knew too well, but a shadow of life. The Church promised you reunion "on some other shore;" but you could hear the doubt in the priest's own voice. Some, in the anguish of such bereavement, have just slowly wilted, then died, not for lack of courage to live alone, but because their life had been so intertwined with that of their partner that the roots of one carried the sustenance of both. Might it be that, when two such partners go beyond this life and into another, they may meet again and recognize the peculiarity of the relationship into which they are entering, not an entirely new one but, rather, one with roots in a previous life? Could this be the "other shore" the Church had promised?

All that may seem fanciful; but some relationships are so deep, so mature, so distinctive, that they are hard to explain in terms of one short life here and now. Indeed, one wonders how two such unlikely people could really endure one another in lifelong marriage with only a few years to prepare them for it. The preparation seems to go deeper, so deep that we say poetically that such marriages must have been "made in heaven." What if they had indeed been made, not in heaven, but in a previous life on earth? Many marriages, and many friendships too, are not at all like that, even the "successful" ones. Some are just the sort that onlookers admire and approve. So also brothers and sisters are often just that: just brothers and sisters having nothing in common but the same paternity and birth in the same womb. Yet now and then is a relationship that has in it a closeness that seems to transcend this life. They are not merely brothers and sisters but soul-mates. More often, however, one finds oneself drawn more to a complete stranger than to one's own kith and kin, sometimes much to the distress of the latter. The Gospel says that to be Christ's disciple one must be completely detached from parents and kin.[3] Though the discovery is peculiarly painful, as is always the sacrifice of the good for the best, the preference is unavoidable. It is the preference for that which transcends this life over that which, however good, is relatively ephemeral.

Do not relationships differ so profoundly in quality as to make one skeptical of the widespread assumption that they are all somehow or other spawned by the same life-situation? Some relationships (the pedestrian ones) reinforce us in the cramping limitations of our life. Others do just the opposite: they lift us out of that prison and lead us into green pastures and still waters that lie beyond it. Is it unthinkable that there might be sometimes a flash of recognition? It would not be a memory of a past life lived together, but something more mysterious still: a glimpse of a past relationship. More wonderful, indeed, than the sense of *déjà vu* is the sense of *déjà connu*.

In a novel about the between-the-wars era in England, the hero, as a result of traumas including an injury in World War I, has lost his memory.[4] The woman who loved him eventually brought his memory back. It was not easy, for such amnesia is not cured in a day. We are not told, indeed, to what extent his memory of the past was recovered. What we *are* told, on the last page, is that there was a flash of recognition, and we are left in no doubt that the power of love was the instrument of transformation. If reincarnation does happen, such flashes of recognition might occur, even though memory of past lives, in the sense in which we ordinarily understand memory, were to be ruled out. *Amor omnia vincit:* love conquers all.

Why, in a reincarnational scheme, should memory be so obliterated? The most obvious answer is that to remember a series of lives would be more than anyone could bear. Even in the course of a single life we mercifully forget much, or at any rate succeed in relegating it to a subconscious level. Following a severe trauma we may suffer an extensive impairment of memory yet function quite well in life. Even those who have forgotten their name, their social identity, and their profession, have not infrequently taken up a new kind of life with considerable poise and much success. That one might forget the details of past lives as a result of the trauma of death and the perhaps still greater trauma of birth, as is symbolized in the Platonic myth by the Waters of Lethe, is surely not inconceivable. At least we may say that it presents no obstacle to belief in a reincarnational scheme. Yet when all that is said, the problem of human relationships of the kind to which I have referred remains. Why should one find a relationship so deep that it seems, even to a skeptic who experiences it, to transcend human life itself, and then, if we assume a reincarnational scheme, forget it in another life, save for these flashes of recognition, these fleeting moments of *déjà connu*? That I should forget, in another life, all acquaintance with, say, the English language, and find myself content to speak instead Hungarian, with German as my second tongue, need not unduly disturb me; but to forget my wife, my mother, my children, and my dearest friends, seems morally offensive.

To such questions the basic answer must be that, for Christians, salvation, like death and birth, is a lonely enterprise. Sustained though I am by the grace of God, and borne up though I be by the faith of the Church, I must work out my "own salvation with fear and trembling."[5] Jesus has provided Christians with the model: it is the loneliness of his Passion and Cross that have opened up the gates of everlasting life. My pilgrimage, for all the dear companions I may meet on the way, is essentially one I must make alone. You can cheer me up; you can tend my blistered feet; you can even carry me over a few rough places; but you can no more do my pilgrimage for me than you can teach me Sanskrit without my learning it. As I must learn alone, no matter how good a teacher I have, so I must walk alone to fulfil my destiny. Nevertheless, these helping hands outstretched on the way play an enormous part in strengthening me, as is attested in the moral codes of all the great religions of the world, Christianity not least. Some friendships are too casual, too fleeting, to make a profound impact on my own psyche; but others are so far-reaching that they must surely be inseparable from the whole development of my being. For all that I must detach myself from dependence on others, I cannot wholly forget those to whom I owe a lifetime of gratitude. In however changed a guise I may encounter them again in the course of my long pilgrimage, there is surely something in them and in me that will ring out loud and clear the signal of re-encounter.

I do not believe we can usefully speculate what, in a reincarnational scheme, it might be. Yet I do not think the notion is entirely unimaginable. I knew, at school, a rather intelligent boy. We were good friends in the general way that schoolboys have of being friends without fuss. We never saw each other after the age of fourteen till, almost exactly thirty years later I happened to be in the city to which he had gone to live. I ascertained his address and looked in on him entirely unannounced. Teasingly, I feigned astonishment that he did not recognize me. I had, of course, the advantage.

"Surely you have not forgotten an old friend?" I said, with all the reproach I could muster.

I knew he was the sort of person who would wish to do his own detective work. I provided no clues. He asked for none. He kept studying my face intently, made a few wildly incorrect guesses, then invited me in for a drink. He asked me to talk about general matters, politics or the weather. He even studied my walk. He was listening and looking so hard that for a moment I thought he might actually hit on my identity. But then, I reflected, he might have forgotten me entirely or, having heard of my doings in adult life, failed to connect them with anyone he had known as a boy. At last he reluctantly gave up. A few clues were enough. Beaming recognition, he said:

"There is absolutely nothing about you that has not changed. You are a completely different person. And yet there's something—something indefinable—well, I just knew we had met, though I could find no reason for supposing it. I thought perhaps if we had a drink together it might help me identify you, but of course it only let me way off the track. Thirty years ago, did you say? Now tell me, honestly, would you have done any better if the shoe had been on the other foot?"

Of course I could have done no better; but though neither of us would have been useful witnesses in a court of law, he had done as well as could be expected in the circumstances. Suppose, however, that not merely thirty years but a whole lifetime had elapsed, and we had found ourselves together in a new life, perhaps on a new planet. Not only could I have no means of stealing a march on him as I did; what would there be to identify? Identification between two such comparatively casual friends might well be impossible; but what if the Brownings were to meet again on Mars? The philosopher may make the obvious objection that there could be nothing at all to enable them to identify each other. What would it *mean* to say the inhabitants of two new bodies could do so? Yet if we are to take seriously at all the notion of reincarnation we may well ask: "What does it *mean* to say that Robert Browning has been reincarnated and Elizabeth Barrett has been reincarnated; they have met; yet they cannot know each other?" A Robert Browning who could not recognize Elizabeth Barrett would not *be* Robert Browning. I think we must either say that reincarnation of the individual cannot occur at all, or else we must say that some recognition, however dim, is not to be excluded.

One of the standard ethical objections to reincarnationism is that the karmic law seems to imply that we are being punished for sins we cannot remember and rewarded for virtues we cannot recall. That is, however, a familiar phenomenon even within one lifetime. Every psychologist knows that I may be "paying" now, in one way or another, for forgotten waywardnesses of my youth. I may also be reaping the fruit of some good thoughts I have long ago put out of my mind, or of some kindly deeds of which I have no longer the slightest recollection. So there can be nothing unethical about my being "punished" for sins I cannot remember or "rewarded" for virtues I cannot recall. For, if I have any personal identity at all, I am still the same person, whether I keep my past actions vividly before my mind or relegate them to a deep drawer in the store room of my unconscious. I could not *be* such a person, however, if I could not, at least in some way, recognize again a "soul-mate" I had once known.

That is, at any rate, a tenable position. Personal identity, as I understand it, *entails* some capacity for such recognition. So a reincarnational eschatology, though it certainly would not provide the instantaneous and full recognition that some dying persons hope for when they say "I shall see him again on the other side," does provide hope of meeting "on some other shore." Moreover, it is not, as I hope to show, incompatible with the more ecstatic hope of final, total recognition in that glorified state in which, Paul says, "I shall know as fully as I am known." [6]

REFERENCES AND NOTES

[1] Mark 12.25.
[2] G. Marcel, *Presence and Immortality* (Pittsburgh, Pennsylvania: Duquesne University Press, 1967).
[3] Luke 14.26.
[4] James Hilton, *Random Harvest* (Boston: Little Brown and Company, 1941).
[5] Philippians 2.12.
[6] I Corinthians 13.12 (J.B.).

XIV

COMMUNICATION WITH
THE DEPARTED

*May the souls of the faithful departed
through the mercy of God, rest in peace.*
Catholic Prayer.

Nothing could be more natural than the wish of a bereaved person to speak with the beloved one who has passed beyond the veil of death. The possibility of such communication has been much discussed during the past hundred years and could not but arouse deep and anguished interest at times such as the aftermath of World War I, when millions of people all over Europe, and many others throughout the world, lost husbands and sweethearts, fathers and sons, brothers and friends, in the terrible carnage of the battlefield. Despite the frowns of conservative churchmen, many people sought, usually through a spiritistic medium, to achieve communication with those who had been taken from them. We must ask whether such communication be possible and, if possible, whether it be desirable for those who walk the Christian Way.

The examination of psychic phenomena has been very seriously undertaken since the foundation, in 1882, of the Society for Psychical Research. A work by one of the founders of that society, F. W. H. Myers, *Human Personality and Its Survival of Bodily Death*, is an early classic in the field, forming part of a vast literature in many languages. Among the many aspects of the Society's investigations, telepathy and hypnotism are two that have produced results so convincing that few who know anything of the kind of evidence that is required and has been adduced can seriously doubt the veracity of the claims of those who engage in such experiments. Other aspects of psychical research, such as motor automation and table-rapping, are much more suspect. Moreover, the inevitable emergence of many fraudulent practitioners, ready to make money out of the grief and distress of the bereaved, complicates the problems further. Still, there remains an element that seems to warrant continued investigation of claims to achieve communication with the dead. Despite the obvious attraction the field offers to impostors and charlatans of every kind, certain phenomena cannot be ignored, great though be the caution that should be exercised in examining them.

In the first place, if we assume that evidence does exist for the presence of phenomena for which no "ordinary scientific explanation" is available, we must ask to what *precisely* the evidence may point. Even a physical phenomenon as commonplace as static electricity, if we knew nothing about electricity, could make plausible the belief that an extraterrestrial intelligent being, or a being in a dimension of existence on this planet but unknown to us, was trying to communicate with us or in some way attract our attention. And, of course, we should be very wrong indeed if we so concluded. All we can say for certain about the kind of phenomena we are now considering is that, in view of what is known for certain about hypnosis and telepathy, for instance, we are not entitled to repudiate out of hand hypotheses in any field of psychic research, except to the extent that there is clear evidence *against* them. That does not take us far, however, toward admitting the possibility of positive communication with such a world beyond the veil of death.

In the second place, the *kind* of alleged communications that purport to come from "the other side" is often so trivial as to raise another, entirely different type of suspicion, namely, that the phenomena are the result of projections from the minds of the assembled members of the *séance*. True, there is no reason, presumably, to expect scintillating wit from such a quarter. Unless the communication purported to come from someone who had been singularly witty, we need not expect unusual brilliance from him in his now allegedly changed state. Nevertheless, if a friend of mine went to Paris or Peking for a week, I should expect more interesting news or comment from him than one generally gets in the course of alleged communications from a spirit world. I find difficulty in imagining that, even if I could go to a dimension of existence beyond the present one and also find a means of returning hither and of communicating with those I had loved before my death, I could have nothing better to say than do the ordinary run of allegedly returning spirits. For the most part these would seem to be talking about such trivia that one wonders why they would go to the trouble of breaking the death-barrier to say so much about so little.

In the third place we are led, therefore, to question anew the possibility of disembodied spirits. In view of the difficulties we have already considered, we must again ask what could be the nature of the focus of a disembodied spirit-energy. Having already considered and repudiated the traditional model of a soul functioning independently from all embodiment, let us now suppose that there may be some focus of spirit-energy that somehow survives the death of the body and awaits re-embodiment. Such a waiting period we may presume to be indefinite: it might be a few years or a thousand. Let us even suppose that such a focus of spirit-energy, even though it could not think or act without embodiment, might nevertheless be capable of reacting to stimuli from individuals who have been in loving relationship with the person whose embodiment the spirit-energy focus has survived. What we know of the strange workings of telepathy and thought-transference, though they do not by any means warrant our making such a hypothesis, do at least make it intelligible.

Having made that very large assumption, we naturally go on to ask what purpose we might hope to achieve by attempting to enter into some form of relationship or communication with the departed. What good might we hope to do? To whom would we be doing it? If such hypothetical foci of spirit-energy exist at all, they exist in an abnormal condition. For, on the reincarnational scheme we are envisioning, they need embodiment for their further development and fulfilment. We must ask, therefore, why we should trouble them. Is not an intrusion on them in their present condition somewhat like disturbing a friend who is asleep in the privacy of his bedroom?

That this is, in fact, very much the sentiment that has prevailed in the Christian Church is easily shown. In the Catholic tradition, prayers to the saints have been not only allowed but encouraged. The practice naturally arose from the strong sense that the Primitive Church had of the Communion of the Saints. The great martyrs and other heroes of the Church, being presumed to have gone to their fulfilment *in patria,* are presumed also to be in a position to help us who are *in via.* So we call on them for their intercession on our behalf or on behalf of someone whom we love. Only those who are believed to be beyond all doubt secure in the possession of their fulfilled state "in heaven" are the proper recipients of such petitions. No such prayers or communications are addressed to the deceased at large. Indeed, in the Roman Catholic system, the processes of beatification and canonization through which such a saint or martyr becomes officially recognized as the proper recipients of prayers are very lengthy and may not even be initiated till years after death. By contrast, one does not pray to the deceased in general; one prays *for* them. The classic form of prayer for the dead is: *requiescant in pace*, may they rest in peace. The most obvious implication is that we wish to save them from all disturbance.

Behind the ancient Catholic formula lies, of course, awareness of a primitive notion of a realm of ghosts who, if provoked into returning, come back to haunt or otherwise trouble the living. Whatever else we do to or for the dead, then, we are not to engage in such ghost-raising. We are to let the departed sleep, to let them rest in peace. We pray for much else for them, of course, for instance, that light may shine eternally upon them and that they may be granted a place of refreshment, even that angels may carry them up to heaven; but undergirding all such prayers is one that is more basic than any of the others: may they rest in peace. As we have already noted, the Primitive Church thought of the departed as "asleep with Christ", awaiting the Day of Judgment. "Asleep in Jesus" is a typical inscription on Christian tombstones and expressive of a deep sentiment that is very Catholic.[1] It is a "Do Not Disturb" sign. We remember the departed in loving prayer, pouring out our hearts for them. We join ourselves mystically with them at Mass as we join ourselves with "the whole company of heaven" including the angels and the seraphim; but we do not attempt to speak to them in such a way as to expect an answer. They are "asleep".

The instinct of the faithful is right. What happens between death and resurrection has always been a perplexing subject for Christians; but the one point on which consensus has always been overwhelming is: the departed, so long as they may be supposed to be in any kind of intermediate state, are not to be disturbed. Besides, a fearsome possibility is not to be ignored, if our inquiry is to be entirely openminded. Disturbing our departed loved ones might not only trouble them but rouse forces hostile to us in some other realm of existence. For if there are such foci of spirit-energy, how can we possibly know enough about them to exclude such a possibility, which, on the assumption we are making for the present purpose, would be very real indeed? The medium's table might turn out to be "a table of devils,"[2] a sinister realm of existence in another dimension that we should be much better off without.

Christians should not ignore the traditional role of the exorcist in the Church, or the fact that Jesus practiced exorcism. That evil influences, too sinister to be entirely accounted for in terms of ordinary kinds of psychology, are active in human society is by no means a hypothesis that can be safely set aside as superstitious humbug. Interest in the subject has been much reawakened in recent years. In England, for instance, the Bishop of Exeter (the late Robert Mortimer) convened a commission to consider the question. He said he had been disturbed both by the hysteria-provoking publicity given to exorcism in the press and by the large number of requests he was receiving for help and advice about exorcizing persons and places. The findings of the Bishop's commission were edited by Dom Robert Petitpierre, O.S.B., and published in a modest and restrained report.[3] This report not only took exorcism very seriously; it recommended the practice of it, with due safeguards, of course, within the life of the Church. It fully recognized, for instance, the possibility that certain places might act as "dispersal centers" for demonic forces. On the very suppositions made by those who believe in foci of spirit-energy, we might be subjecting not only ourselves but our beloved ones to such infinitely terrible and fearsome evil agencies.

That reflection leads us to another, very different consideration. To pray for the dead whom we have loved is obviously what any Christian is inclined to do; but what motive could one have for trying to communicate with them? Could it be other than a selfish motive? No ordinarily considerate person would be so callous and so selfish as deliberately to disturb a friend who, after a heavy day's work, was in a sound sleep. Would anyone pretend that loneliness was an excuse for such conduct? Surely only the most neurotic and self-centered people would ever do anything of the sort. Even in the loneliness that bereavement can bring, which is surely one of the most terrible forms of human anguish, one could think of troubling the departed only through extreme selfish indifference to their welfare. The suggestion that the departed wish to communicate with us but cannot do so because we are insensitive to them or fail to put ourselves in the way of receiving messages they might wish to send carries no weight with the Christian. For Christians who engage in prayer, especially during the celebration of the Mass, the focal point of Catholic worship, are as sensitive to spiritual communication as ever they could be. If a departed spirit wished to communicate with such a prayerful Christian, that spirit would surely be able to make use of such a perfect opportunity. No, nothing but selfishness could impel anyone to intrude upon the privacy of a presumptively disembodied spirit. To be open and receptive to communication that might come to us from "the other side" is, of course, a different matter.

Spiritists claim that such spirits are capable of "materialization", assuming corporeal forms or using other material instrumentalities on a temporary, *ad hoc* basis. Such a notion is open to precisely the kind of objections we have already considered. But what dangers inhere in compelling or cajoling such entities to manifest themselves! Moreover, what motive other than selfishness would impel one to elicit such "temporary materialization"?

The heart that has emptied itself in love for another person will not readily so disturb the peace of the beloved. However bitter the grief, however sore the distress, however terrible the anguish of the bereavement, the last thing a true lover will do is to trouble his or her beloved. A true lover who believes in any kind of afterlife will be ever-waiting for opportunity to meet the beloved again. Such waiting-ness is part of the conviction that sustains the Christian in hope. The last thing he would do is to run even the risk of impeding the re-embodiment (and consequent opportunities for further growth) of the beloved person.

I often think of a widow, a deeply convinced, and very intelligent Christian who, by the way, had inclinations to some form of reincarnationist belief, and who, in the depth of her anguish, prayed many times daily that she might hear just once again one word in the voice of her deceased husband. Weeks passed. No sign or sound came to her that she could conceivably interpret as an answer to her prayer. Her practice, which she continued for the remaining thirty-six years of her life, was to visit her husband's grave every Sunday afternoon. A few months after his death, when her anguish was at its worst, she was on her weekly pilgrimage when suddenly she felt a strong impulse to visit the grave of an acquaintance. The impulse seemed irrational, since she had no particular interest in that other person or his family, nor had she heard from them for many years. When she came to the grave, she noticed that the stone had been cleaned and that another name had been added, a name she did not even know. Also added were the newly inscribed words: "With Christ far better." These words suddenly captured her. She saw them as a direct answer to her search. A great peace came over her, a peace which, she told me many years later, never left her. It seems to me that that is, to say the least, a more likely way for God to exercise his care over those who love much. In such ways comes what Christians call "the peace of God which passeth all understanding."[4]

REFERENCES AND NOTES

[1]Though *dormit in pace* ("he/she sleeps in peace") is extremely common, ejaculatory prayers such as *vivas vincas* ("may you live; may you conquer") and *deus tibi refrigeret* ("may God refresh you") also occur. (The practice of adding such prayers was derived from pre-Christian custom.) From a reincarnationist standpoint, by no means the least interesting of such phrases is one that occurs in an inscription in the Galleria Lapidaria, a collection of classical and early Christian epigraphical material founded by Pope Clement XIV and housed in the Vatican Museum. In an epitaph for Marcus, "an innocent boy" (*puer innocens*), we find: QVAM TELETVM EXCIPET MATER ECLESIAE DEOC MVNDO REVERTENTEM ("How gladly will Mother Church receive you, returning from/to this world").

The collection is catalogued by O. Marucchi, *Collezione di epigrafi. Guida speciale della Galleria Lapidaria de Museo Vaticano.* Rome, 1912. For the catalogue reference I am indebted to my colleague, Dr. Susan V. Lenkey.

[2]I Corinthians 10.21.

[3]Robert Petitpierre, *Exorcism* (London: Society for Promoting Christian Knowledge, 1972).

[4]On the subject of this chapter, *see also* a contribution by the present writer to Ronald Selby Wright, ed., *Asking Them Questions,* New Series, Part II (London: Oxford University Press, 1972), pp.62-70. To avoid misunderstanding, however, I would affirm my belief that we should never close our minds to possible communication *from* the departed.

XV

REINCARNATION AND THE WAR BETWEEN MYSTICISM AND FAITH

> *For I am not ashamed of the Good News . . . it shows how faith leads to faith, or as scripture says: The upright man finds life through faith.*
>
> Paul, *Letter to the Romans,* quoting the prophet Habakkuk

> *I know a man in Christ who, fourteen years ago . . . was caught up into paradise and heard things which must not and cannot be put into human language.*
>
> Paul, *Second Letter to the Corinthians*

> *Mysticism and historical revelation mutually exclude one another so forcibly that a mixture of them destroys both.*
>
> Friedrich Gogarten, *Die Religiöse* Entscheidung

Mysticism and reincarnationism tend to flourish together. The reason is, of course, that they are both historically associated with the notion that the soul is immortal because it is in one way or another a spark of the divine fire. That notion has been unequivocally rejected by all orthodox Christians and is not generally favored even among the vaguely heterodox. Therefore, wherever mysticism has sprouted in the garden of the Christian Church, it has always been suspect as an alien weed. It has sprouted, nevertheless, in some profusion. Some of its exponents have exposed themselves to the charge of pantheism; but the most interesting Christian mystics have generally been at pains to avoid it. John of the Cross, for instance, says that, when the soul rises high on the rugged slopes of Carmel, it finds God and is bound to God by a cord of love (*hilo de amor*), remaining different in substance but *as* one in love. While the soul *appears* to be fused with God it is not in fact so; it only appears so because of the grip of the *hilo*.[1] The soul, rapt in mystical ecstasy of love of God, *feels* as if fused with God; yet the gulf between God and man, so characteristic of the three great monotheistic religions, Judaism, Christianity, and Islam, is preserved.

Whenever the category of faith dominates the religious scene, as it does wherever biblical tradition is normative, mysticism is suspect, for mysticism implies that direct, immediate contact with God that seems to make faith unnecessary. When you are waiting at the airport for an old friend, you wait in faith that he will not let you down; but when he arrives and you greet one another, what need can you have at that moment for such faith? The mystic, if he takes mystical experience to be the norm of the religious life, is claiming that, though there may be occasional times when God disappears so that one needs faith to carry one over these dark periods, the ideal, if not the normal, religious life is one of such close walking with God that faith can be viewed as a second-order religious exercise.

Reincarnationism, apart from the traditional suspicions that attend it in Christian circles, by reason of its association with heretical groups, shares with mysticism a susceptibility to the two following objections: (1) it is associated with a pantheistic attitude toward God and the soul; (2) claiming "sight", it purports, at least implicitly, to be able to dispense with faith. War between faith and mysticism within the Christian Church is, therefore, highly relevant to our study of the grounds on which reincarnationism might be brought within the scope of the Christian Way. Catholic tradition is more hospitable to mysticism than is Protestantism; yet even Catholic sentiment is distrustful of it. Thomas Aquinas ac-

counted mystical experience a fleeting foretaste of the Beatific
Vision of heaven. It is not to be sought after; nevertheless, if it
comes to a person, it should be received with gratitude (though
also always with extreme caution), as a sign of exceptional divine
favor. The Protestant tradition is much more uncompromisingly
hostile, at least in theory, though in some forms of Protestantism
mystical experiences do sometimes succeed in gaining, if precari-
ously, a slender foothold.

Kierkegaard (1813-1855), one of the greatest religious geniuses
in human history, was extraordinarily opposed to mysticism,
which he associated with the aestheticism in religion that he very
properly trounced as a spectator sport masquerading as religious
activity. Kierkegaard, himself a child of the age of Romanticism,
saw the greatness and the weakness of that great nineteenth century movement. He admired Mozart's *Don Giovanni* as an expression of the finest in opera. He loved art and culture. He saw the
Christian Way, however, as diametrically opposed to them. They
are essentially, in his view, narcissistic. It is pleasant to look in the
mirror, especially if one can find a flattering mirror. Art, he thinks,
panders to this very natural human inclination. It helps one to
luxuriate and delight in one's own being. It enables one to flee from
relationships and (as so often we say without apology) simply
enjoy oneself. The cultivated man can use his fine taste to enjoy a
richer, fuller, more delicate aesthetic experience than the ordinary
ruck of mankind can hope to attain. The mystic, according to
Kierkegaard, merely carries the refinement a step further, enlist-
ing not only opera and painting, poetry and architecture, in the
service of his narcissistic pleasure, but God. He is a Don Juan so
irrevocably committed to his self-centeredness that even God
becomes part of his exquisite game. He really worships himself,
this pretend-religious Don Juan, and therefore can never rest till he
persuades himself that he has captured God and enlisted him into
the ministry of his own narcissism. The narrowness of Kierkegaard's notion of mysticism is generally taken to be due to his
having received most of his information about it from the romantic
thinker Franz von Baader, from Josef von Görres, the author of a
well-known work on Christian mysticism, and from the Romantic
novels that were flooding Europe. Schleiermacher, who described
religion in terms of feeling, Chateaubriand, who proclaimed the
doctrine that even if Christianity were rooted in falsehood it would
still be valuable because of the fine culture it had brought about,

and (nearer our own day) Santayana, who did not take religion seriously at all yet so much loved the rhythm and charm of Catholic ritual and practice that in his last years he stayed with the Blue Nuns in Rome so that he might savor the delights of a Catholic ambience: these typify the sort of attitude Kierkegaard deplored in religion, and with which he associated mysticism. He was right, of course, in respect of a great deal of phony mysticism, which is pure narcissism of the most spiritually debilitating kind; but one does not judge anything by caricatures of it, nor does one appraise any virtue by the hypocrites whose hypocrisy pays tribute to it.

His view is eloquently expressed in one of his writings in which he clearly wishes us to understand that mysticism is worse than paganism.[2] "The fault of the mystic is that by his choice he does not become concrete for himself, nor for God either; he chooses himself abstractly and therefore lacks transparency. For it is a mistake to think that the abstract is the transparent. The abstract is the turbid, the foggy. Therefore, his love for God reaches its highest expression in a feeling, a mood: in the dusk of the evening when fogs prevail he melts with vague movements into one with his God."[3] He likens the mystic to a person who, having once fallen in love, thinks he has nothing to do but wait to see if it will come again in just as much glory. This attitude he contrasts with that of the man who finds the religious significance of life in doing his duty. The knight of faith, whom Kierkegaard upholds as the true Christian, is the one who has made the right choice. In contrast to the Alexandrians and others who, in the ancient Church, were comparatively hospitable to Gnostic notions and tended, therefore, to account faith a stepping-stone to the knowledge (*gnosis*) that transcends it, Kierkegaard proclaims faith superior to knowledge. In taking this stance he is sure to sound absurd to those who, thinking of faith as belief, inevitably regard it as a weak sort of knowledge, never to be desired except when one has nothing better to take its place. Kierkegaard, however, intends by "faith" something very different. He means, rather, an attitude more akin to that of the enterprising scientist who ventures out into the realm of the unknown, risking his energy, time, and skill on a hypothesis. The knight of faith, like such a scientist, uses an inductive other than a deductive method and, above all, he exercises moral qualities, not least courage. In respect to the afterlife, all this acquires special significance. Not only reincarnationism but all specification of the nature of heaven, hell, and purgatory, are ruled out. We

are called to walk in faith, not to pretend to sight. We may believe
in a fuller and better life beyond the grave, but in what way it is to
be fuller and better is not a proper speculation. Not only is it futile;
it is specifically forbidden. Reincarnation is therefore simply not a
topic for a Christian to consider or discuss.

Kierkegaard's extreme opposition to the kind of climate of
thought in which reincarnation might be entertained by Christians
is understandable, in view of the extraordinarily limited and indeed
mistaken notions he had about a mystical approach to religion. In
the Protestant heritage he is, however, by no means unique.
Albrecht Ritschl (1822-89) held mysticism to be *unterchristlich,*
inferior to and incompatible with Christianity. Wilhelm Herrmann
(1846-1922), Ritschl's disciple, went even beyond his master in
excluding mysticism from religion.[4] The life of faith, he taught,
leaves no room at all for the kind of experiences to which mysticism appeals. Herrmann also excluded metaphysical inquiry from
the life of faith, which he held to be directed solely to the life of the
historical Christ, yet only to the extent that that life possesses
ethical value relevant to the believer. Friedrich Gogarten is even
more explicit, teaching that attempts to keep both faith and mysticism (as if one did not have to choose between them) end in
emptying both of their content. For Gogarten they are mutually
exclusive. The whole theological school of Karl Barth, which
exercised unparalleled influence on conservative Protestantism
between World Wars I and II was radically opposed to mysticism.
Emil Brunner, an ardent supporter of that school, though he departed from Barth on certain points, expresses the ground of its
opposition: while the mystics seek fusion with God, the Bible
always insists on the gulf between God and man.[5] God always
remains *ganz anders, totaliter aliter,* wholly other. Mysticism, the
Barthians felt, put in jeopardy that fundamental relationship of
faith.

That has been, in fact, a typically cavalier assumption within
that climate of Protestant thought. Not only are Catholics more
hospitable to mysticism and "liberal" Protestants more tolerant of
it; Judaism and Islam, the two other great monotheistic religions of
the world that both certainly share, if they do not traditionally
outdo, Christian insistence on the gulf between God and man, are
by no means inhospitable to mysticism, as the presence of Has-
sidism and Sufism attests. All three religions are religions of faith.
Their adherents are all at least spiritual descendants of Abraham,

that great exemplar of faith, who "set out without knowing where he was going."[6] Paul did not find faith and mysticism mutually exclusive. On the contrary, while he proclaims with the prophet Habakkuk that the upright man finds life through faith, he is nothing if not a mystic.[7] He speaks over and over again of being "in Christ" and uses imagery and concepts typical of the great mystical writers of all ages. The language he uses of Baptism and the Eucharist reflect his attitude. We have been buried with Christ, united in death with him, and we are to be united with him in a resurrection like his.[8] His relationship with Christ, from his conversion on the Damascus Road, involved ecstatic experiences. In his second letter to the Corinthians he tells of being "caught up . . . into the third heaven . . . caught up into paradise," where he heard things "which must not and cannot be put into human language."[9] Professor W. D. Davies observes that Paul, though he mentions such experiences, makes clear that he does not overrate their importance, for he knew the dangers of mysticism.[10] The reminder is salutary; nevertheless, nothing is clearer than that Paul was able to combine the life of faith with mystical vision.

That combination is precisely what is needed for the christening of karma. Only through a false *gnosis*, bolstered by an idle luxuriating in self-induced ecstatic experiences masquerading as mystical encounter with God, do we ever dare to talk glibly of a chain of reincarnation as though we could know the range of our destiny as God knows it. We cannot pretend to leap out of the bonds of this life and truly encompass what lies beyond it. We can no more pretend to know the geography of the afterlife than we can claim to know our history in a pre-existent one. Indeed, the presuppositions of a karmic doctrine should make us very chary about all such enterprises, for the fulfilment of karma in any life demands that we give our full attention to the here-and-now problems with which it confronts us. We should look on life as a struggle, not as a hymn. Nevertheless, if the divine music does break in upon us while we are walking in faith, are we to turn a deaf ear to it? Of course not. It is God's preview of his intentions for us: not enough to enable us to write God's script for him; just enough to sustain us as we trudge along.

Indeed, only the knight of faith knows how to cope with such occasional glimpses, such intimations of the afterlife, such re-membrances of pre-existence. When you are, as is he, in the midst of battle, you can feel in no danger of luxuriating in narcissistic folly if, for a fleeting instant, when your heart is pounding in terror and your hand trembling with fright, you catch a strain of angel voices or see a glimpse of paradise. Only the knight of faith can be sure of the authenticity of such visions as may be vouchsafed to him. Faith itself implies a claim to a certain *kind* of knowledge as much as it entails a confession of a peculiarly enlightened form of ignorance. As Father Holloway reminds us at the end of a thoughtful book, "Faith is not a possession or a privilege; it is a way of seeing, a recognition."[11] Yet it is a unique way of seeing, an unparalleled kind of recognition. For it comes through action more than from reflection. Unlike the belief that epistemologists contrast with knowledge, it is "distinguished from the entertainment of a probable proposition by the fact that the latter can be a completely theoretic affair. Faith is a 'yes' of self-commitment. . . ."[12]

There is nothing in faith or in the life of faith that need exclude reincarnationism as a way of understanding human destiny. The most learned and perspicacious of Christian theologians have always seen heaven and hell as, in one way or another, symbols of states of consciousness, rather than abodes, as they are in primitive thought. Why, then, may they not be accounted aspects of the road we call the afterlife? Do not we find them, indeed, aspects of the road we call our present life? What is traditionally called purgatory or "the intermediate state", whose nature the learned in the Church have been generally even more reluctant to specify, is then open to a reincarnationist interpretation along the lines already considered in a previous chapter.

The following model might be proposed. In the Canon of the Mass, according to both Roman and Anglican usage, at the Commemoration for the Departed, the celebrating priest prays for those who have gone before us with the sign of faith (*cum signo fidei*) and are now sleeping the sleep of peace (*dormiunt in somno pacis*). After a brief silent prayer for the persons he intends to be specifically remembered, the priest goes on to ask that they and "all who rest in Christ" (*omnibus in Christo quiescentibus*) be granted "a place of refreshment, of light, and of peace" (*locum refrigerii, lucis et pacis*). But if they are now sleeping peacefully and at rest "in Christ", whither can they be bound? If it be heaven, why not say so? There could be nothing improper in asking that those for whom we are praying should find their way as soon as possible to heaven, if that is what we have in mind for them.

Certainly it cannot be that we are asking that they be sent to hell. Then can it be purgatory, the anteroom to heaven? No, for whatever purgatory may be, it cannot surely be described as a place of refreshment, or of light, or of peace. So we are not asking any of the conventional, traditional things for our beloved departed. We are leaving the whole matter open, as is the Church's custom when she is at her wisest. We are assuming that they are at rest in Christ, and we are asking that, when they awake from that rest, from which we have no intention of disturbing them, they will find themselves in a salutary condition. Refreshment, light, and peace are the circumstances necessary for moral and spiritual growth, and for the conduct of useful and profitable labor. They are circumstances incompatible with both purgatory and heaven, as traditionally understood by the popular imagination, but eminently compatible with both purgatory and heaven when understood as dimensions of the afterlife. That is to say, they are compatible with reincarnation, whether on earth or on some other planet.

Walking in faith as we do, we ought not to claim to designate with any greater precision the nature of human destiny, or to chart the course of our human pilgrimage as children of God. All we dare say is that, while we "know not where his islands lift their fronded palms in air," we do see, though "in a glass, darkly," that our lives stretch beyond the frontiers of birth and death that enclose us in our present life. We see, too, that, because God is infinitely good, and we are far from attaining our full capacity as moral and spiritual beings, we may hope to be granted further opportunities for growth. Since the whole of the New Testament witness stresses the promise of resurrection, reincarnation becomes an appropriate vehicle of that promise. We can claim no more. Yet when we consider the formal alternatives available to Christian faith, the plausibility of a reincarnationist view is certainly by no means diminished.

Before we leave this topic for our concluding chapter, I would make a plea on behalf of our treatment of the dying and those who mourn their passing. Three general conclusions emerge from our study: (1) Christians must walk in faith, for they do not claim any exact knowledge about the details of the afterlife; (2) the Christian traditions about the afterlife are in a state of extreme confusion, and (3) reincarnationism is not incompatible with Christian faith. In view of these conclusions, I think we must take very seriously possibilities such as I have proposed: at death the energy of the person does not disperse but its focus enters into a period of rest or sleep, after which it chooses (subject to the karmic limitations imposed upon it) a new birth such as will best serve its particular needs for development and growth. On this view, as I have suggested, purgatory and heaven intertwine as dimensions of the afterlife. If, then, that picture of the afterlife is even plausible, surely we must drastically revise the kind of preparation for death that is customarily given in Western society. Surely we ought to take account, at least, of the possibility that the customary preparation may be singularly unsuitable and that a very different one may be what the dying person needs.

Clergymen, unless they are extraordinarily ignorant of the difficulties attending Christian traditions about the afterlife, are usually at least a little embarrassed in approaching the subject at all. What can they say beyond the generalizations and platitudes of theological boilerplate? There is a happy land beyond the grave? There may be a period of preparation in purgatory before one gets to heaven, and so we shall pray for the repose of the soul of the dying person so that he or she may pass as swiftly as possible through that fiery ordeal and come speedily into the delight of being for ever close to God in heaven? That they are about to pass over in one giant leap into the fuller presence of God?

To make such suggestions may not be entirely wrong, since of course, on the view I am proposing as a possibility, they do in some way symbolize what may lie in store for those who are about to die. Yet if my proposal were closer to the facts than are any of the more usual ways of symbolizing the afterlife within the Christian tradition, then surely these suggestions would constitute uncommonly roundabout, not to say distorted, ways of delineating what the dying person should be encouraged to expect. Should not one at least tell such a person of that possibility?

Many people, perhaps especially among those who have labored at dreary chores most of their lives, long above all for rest. They sympathize with the old woman who told her friends:

> Don't mourn for me now, don't mourn for me never:
> Ah's gone to do nothin' for ever an' ever.

So we can assure those who die in Christ that, at least according to one view, they are about to fall asleep in Christ and so to rest till they are sufficiently refreshed to be ready for the next stage, which some take to be the exciting adventure of a rebirth. Should not the dying give some thought, at least, to that possibility, so that they may direct their attention to some of its possible consequences? Others who, like Lloyd George, are seriously oppressed by the notion that heaven, whither they are hopefully bound, is to be a state of endless hymn-singing, could be assured that the prospect is indeed far more exciting. So, as the dying pass beyond us, in faith that beside them are their Lord's staff and rod, to hearten them, they may find solace and joy in such an interpretation of the road they are to travel with their Lord, who by his own Resurrection has made such a prospect infinitely more exciting and fulfilling, since it confers on them the assurance of his continual sustenance and care.[13]

For the bereaved and those who dread impending bereavement, the consequences of such a view of the afterlife would be hardly less considerable. Not only would they be more inclined to let the departed rest in peace; they could wish them also *bon voyage* in the Lord. Many times have I heard a dying person whisper: "Pray for me: I am going on a long journey." Now we could take that as a flash of deep insight. Instead of greeting it with platitudes that cannot but seem irrelevant if the insight be genuine, we could not only nod and smile our cordial concurrence but remind our brother or sister that the journey will not be a solitary one, nor even an entirely unfamiliar one, since he who has walked with them in this life will continue to walk with them every step of the way in the life beyond. They will be walking alone only in the sense in which they have always walked alone, that is, because God who loves his children lets them so walk because he lets them be and, in letting them be, lets them grow;[14] so that they may be, in the words of Charles Wesley's hymn, "changed from glory into glory." That such a prospect is more *palatable* to many, both among the dying and among those who mourn them, does not, of course, make it true. That it is a more *intelligible* prospect should be, however, an important as well as a commendable consideration.

REFERENCES AND NOTES

[1]Juan de la Cruz, *Cantico espiritual,* 31, *anotación,* Vol. 2, (*Obras,* Toledo edit., 1912 ff), p. 324.

[2]S. Kierkegaard, *Either/Or,* Vol. 2, tr. W. Lowrie (Princeton, N.J.: Princeton University Press, 1971), p. 244.

[3]Ibid., p. 252.

158   REINCARNATION IN CHRISTIANITY

Christian with God.) 1866.

[5] See *Die Mystik und das Wort* (1924).

[6] Hebrews: 11.8.

[7] Romans: 1.17; Habakkuk: 2.4.

[8] Romans: 6.5.

[9] II Corinthians: 12.2-4.

[10] W. D. Davies, *Invitation to the New Testament* (New York: Doubleday Anchor Books edition, 1969), p. 347.

[11] Richard Holloway, *New Vision of Glory* (New York: Seabury Press, 1974), p. 194.

[12] Dorothy Emmet, *The Nature of Metaphysical Thinking* (New York: St. Martin's Press, 1945), p. 140.

[13] Psalm: 23.4 (JB).

[14] *See* G. MacGregor, *He Who Lets Us Be* (New York: Seabury Press, 1975).

XVI

A NEW VISION
OF THE AFTERLIFE

> *In my Father's house are many man-*
> *sions....I go to prepare a place for you.*
>
> John:14.2.

In this concluding chapter I wish to present a vision of the afterlife
such as will show how reincarnationism could not only fit into but
clarify Christian hope concerning human destiny.

Once again we must be on our guard. We must be careful not to
mistake the nature of our undertaking. If we expect "proof",
either as in a theorem in geometry or as in an experiment in
chemistry, we shall certainly be disappointed. I do not believe
such proof possible in respect of either the existence or the nature
of God, and since the possibility of an afterlife depends on both
God's existence and his nature, such a proof about anything relating to an afterlife is, in my view, out of the question. If one is not
persuaded of the possibility of some kind of afterlife, no logical or
scientific method could conceivably lead to belief in it. Such a
conclusion can spring only from faith. Nevertheless, the man or
woman who walks in faith rightly seeks to articulate that faith
intelligibly. The extraordinarily muddled state of traditional Christian eschatology serves only to perplex those who so live by
Christian faith. Our task is to try to provide a more intelligible
account of that to which Christian faith and hope point.

159

First, I think we should recognize with Paul that there is nothing intrinsically immortal in a human being as such. The doctrine, indisputably a part of both Jewish and Christian orthodoxy, that man is made in the image of God does not necessarily imply that individual human beings may not die like dogs. I can see no sound biblical or other reason for believing in the imperishability of the individual as such. All creation is made in the image of God in some degree. Humanity is no more than a special case eminently show-ing forth that image. So I can see no reason why John Smith or Mary Jones may not die, and in their dying be extinguished for ever. When a person spends an entire lifetime thinking and talking of nothing but stocks and bonds, clothes and booze, and other ministrations to self-centeredness, one may well wonder what purpose another lifetime of the same could serve. If, however, one were to return thousands of times, begin all over again, perhaps even in another galaxy, and still fail to grow in any direction no matter what kind of soil or sunshine or rain might be provided for one's growth, surely nothing in the economy of the cosmos could be served by the continuation of the futile process. That such an outcome is to be expected in many cases seems to me a conclusion both grounded in Scripture and suggested by everyday obser-vation. When people are patently so purblind as to walk daily past Jacob's ladder with a yawn and sit over and over again within earshot of angelic choirs, all while talking of their golf scores and of ways of arranging bridge parties, their case seems as hopeless as that of a graduate student in mathematics who has never really mastered the multiplication table.

Nevertheless, wherever there is even a slight stirring of the spirit of man, a movement, however feeble, toward fuller life, a flow, however trickling, of compassion and human understanding, or even so much as a desperate ambition to get somehow beyond the prison of one's own circumstances and the straightjacket of one's own mind, then another chance is what one would expect of the God of love. Even the most rigorous professional examinations, which impose strict time-limits, provide for more than one chance. In case of failure, one may try again. Christian tradition has recog-nized such a notion in the Catholic doctrine of purgatory, surely one of the most consoling as well as morally invigorating doctrines in all Christian teaching. In this life I get but one sheet of paper to work out the equation assigned to me. I try. I do not entirely botch it; yet, when the bell rings, my work is far from finished. That may well be largely my own fault. I wasted much time day-dreaming. Besides, I had allowed my mind to become blocked in several ways. As the bell rings I know I have not passed, yet I have reason to believe that if only I could try all over again I could solve the equation and so qualify for the next stage of my career. I have not been cowardly or dishonest. I have not walked out on the whole thing in disgust. I certainly have not tried to cheat. When, afterwards, I go over the paper with my teacher, he assures me that what I need is more practice in taking examinations, in working under examination conditions. Next time, he says encouragingly, I have a ninety per cent chance of passing. Is not that the situation of the majority of examinees at a first try in any worthwhile examination? It is the sort of real-life situation to which, *mutatis mutandis*, the doctrine of purgatory addresses itself.

That doctrine of purgatory, emerging as it did in a mass of mental confusion about the destiny of man, was vague and ambiguous from the start.[1] Even for those simple souls who thought of heaven as a shining city in the sky approached by pearly gates, paved with gold and watered by crystal rivers, as they thought of hell as a burning dungeon below, the concept of purgatory was inchoate. Sometimes people thought of it as a pale version of hell; but then they saw that would not do, because, being a correctional rather than a penal institution, every flame has a cleansing and clarifying purpose. In hell, on the contrary, the bitterest pill is the awareness that nothing ever does any good to anybody. Nothing can ever be accomplished in hell, for purpose itself has been for ever abolished. Then, to the eyes of faith, purgatory is a pilgrimage much more like that of this life than either heaven or hell could ever be.

Then why should not it be precisely that? Apart from the prejudices against reincarnationism that we have already considered, a further, theological objection must have presented itself to the thoughtful. The resurrection of the dead was generally supposed to take place "in the end" when the whole universe was about to be "rolled up like a scroll" and time itself about to terminate. So in purgatory souls must be in a disembodied state and the purgatorial process, therefore, adapted to that condition. Yet the notion of such a condition of spiritual disembodiment was as alien to the Aristotelian philosophy and science of the Middle Ages as it is to contemporary science and philosophy. So purgatory remained the fuzzy notion it had ever been and the Latin mania for legalistic definition served only to aggravate the fuzziness. That is one reason, of course, why it remained so susceptible, as notoriously it was, to the crass abuses of the late Middle Ages. Souls in purgatory were depicted as in flames, leaping forward in their anguish toward that state in which they hoped eventually to be pure enough to enter God's living room. Prayers would help them. Holy Mass, being the appropriation of the infinite merits of Christ, would help infinitely; yet a thousand masses were generally taken to be a thousand times better for them than one, though one mass is held to be infinite in efficacy. The heirs of the Reformation, because of such abuses, abandoned the whole idea of an intermediate state, leaving themselves with an even more unintelligible eschatology.

If we are to accept the notion of an intermediate or purgatorial state at all, a form of reincarnation would fit the case perfectly. It need not wholly exclude a quiescent interval between incarnations, for we know far too little of the nature of psychic energy to know how that might or might not work. Reincarnationism would dispose, however, of the notion of an indefinitely disembodied soul leaping about and hoping that the next celebration of mass at St. Aloysius Church might take the form of a requiem for him (while mentally noting that even a mere "special intention" at mass would be better than no mass at all), thought of course a whole novena of masses, or even a mass "in perpetuity," could do nothing to expedite the Day of Judgment and the consequent return of his duly glorified body. Surely purgatory, whatever it be, must be more adventuresome than that.

In an earlier chapter I suggested that some people, when they hear of an idea such as I am suggesting, that purgatory may consist in our rebirth, exclaim half in jest: "Oh, not *again*! I thought this *was* purgatory!" Of course, on the view I am proposing, they would be perfectly right. This life would be part of the long and arduous process of evolutionary moral growth that purgatory must surely be by any reckoning. One must be born again in the flesh or in some other embodiment in order that the birth of the spirit may be gradually achieved. Otherwise, why are we born in the flesh even once?

Then is the process of growth to go on interminably? Is what the Tractarians called "the intermediate state" really no intermediate state at all but the normal state of affairs in the cosmos? If, as Origen and others have suggested, God creates eternally, then the notion that growth (which implies temporal duration) might go on interminably is plausible, in the sense that it is not self-contradictory. Nor is the notion of an eternal creating as patently contrary to Scripture as the classic theologians in the West have generally assumed. For while Greek and Latin translations of Genesis use a "past definite" or "perfect" form of the verb "to create" (*In principio creavit Deus caelum et terram*), the Hebrew language, having a different verb structure, has no means of being so specific.[2] So even a biblical literalist cannot rightly insist as strongly as has been traditional on the notion that God is not always creating.

Nevertheless, there is another objection (in my view a much more serious one) to the suggestion that the process of growth might go on interminably: it seems contrary to all Christian philosophies of history. That the main stream of Christian tradition has envisioned an *eschaton*, an end that is to come about somehow or other, whether on a specific Day of Judgment or otherwise, is indisputable. Indeed, even those generally accounted at variance with that main stream of Christian tradition have expected the process to end. Origen, for instance, looked forward to an apocatastasis, an end that would bring final salvation for all, even Satan. Universalists, Moravians, Christadelphians, and others nearer our own time who have repudiated the notion of hell have none the less envisioned a culmination of the process of life and growth in which we now find ourselves. Moreover, if we are willing to look to other religions, we find counterparts to such an idea. Mahayana Buddhists, seeing the cycle of births as a painful process from which they are eventually to be delivered through entry into nirvanic bliss, may even entertain the hope that, if only one is saintly enough, one may not have to return to earth at all but be plunged into nirvanic bliss at the moment of death. In some forms of Buddhism occurs even the notion that one may choose to return as a benevolent *bodhisattva* to help one's fellows, though one is under no compulsion to do so. Though the traditional Christian view envisions, of course, a different sort of heavenly bliss, the expectation of an end to the process is common to both systems. Might a Christian repudiate an expectation that is not only widespread in the history of the religions of the world but also indisputably central to his own tradition? What, indeed, would it mean to speak of a process without speaking also of a fulfilment?

True, process and growth, as we understand them, do entail fulfilment. The seed becomes a flower; the shoot becomes a tree;

the child becomes a man. All that is fulfilment: the fulfilment of biological process. The process of mental and spiritual development entails fulfilment too; but need it, indeed could it, be expected to be of the same kind? Are the mental and moral qualities that I have gone on developing long after I stopped "growing up" to attain some day their full stature as I once attained my full physical stature of seventy-one inches? Is the love of God of such a character that one could ever say, "I have now reached the fulfilment of my potential in loving God," as one can say "I have reached my full stature of seventy-one inches"? I find such a notion difficult to invest with meaning. It would seem to me that the fulfilment of my creaturely being as a moral, intellectual, and spiritual entity, cannot be at all of the same order as biological fulfilment. The difference seems to me to be somewhat like the difference between kindness and a helping of potatoes. To the question, "Would you like more potatoes?" I may well reply, "No, thank you, I have enough" or, if I were to be more physiologically specific, "No, thank you, my digestion is limited in capacity." No one could ever so respond to the question, "Would you like some more kindness?" To that, of course, I would say, rather, something such as, "Indeed, I hope that no one's kindness will ever stop, but that, on the contrary, it may be ever enhanced. Of course I can never have enough of yours, thank you." The fulfilment of a Christian's destiny may have been conceived too much on the model of the fulfilment of biological growth: a hidden category confusion.

The notion that an individual human being, having attained the plenitude of his or her moral and spiritual development, should continue to enjoy moral and spiritual maturity and exercise it after all growth and development had ceased is to me unintelligible. It would seem like a suggestion that an animal, having attained full stature, ceased to move. For to be a moral being *is* to have engaged in a development and growth that have no meaning apart from the process of that growth and that development. Everything that invests life with the kind of meaning that religious people attribute to their lives is of such a character that the meaning evaporates as soon as we try to talk about the attainment of moral and spiritual perfection, as though we were talking about the completion of a building. Yet that is precisely the model traditionally used by Christians, both on the popular and on the learned level, for the notion of heaven. Even the concept of the Beatific Vision as the medieval theologians presented it (a state in which the beatified soul, having attained perfect knowledge of God, enjoys God for ever, being therefore completely happy) provides no definite notion of growth. No wonder that Lloyd George, in his recollections of a Baptist upbringing over a hundred years ago, could honestly say that the thought of heaven as a place of "perpetual Sundays with perpetual services" frightened him more than the thought of hell, nearly driving him mad and making him for ten years an atheist. To be a perfectly moral and spiritual being yet not be able to grow could only be conceived, if indeed it could be conceived at all, as somewhat like being a perfect dog who nevertheless could not run or wag his tail.

To be capable of the Beatific Vision is to be capable of "seeing" God perfectly. We recall the ingenuity of Thomas Aquinas' reply to those who objected that the beatified in heaven, being of different degrees of holiness, must be of correspondingly different degrees of happiness and therefore could not all be perfectly happy: Thomas replied that they are like cups of different sizes but each cup perfectly full. The reply was characteristically discerning; nevertheless, while it deals admirably with the question as posed, it takes no account of the difficulty with which we are now concerned. Heaven, whatever it be, cannot be *totally* different from human consciousness on earth, the earth on which, according to Christian orthodoxy, God chose to pitch his tent among us. If we may speak, as do some of the Christian mystics, of a foretaste on earth of heavenly bliss, we cannot (even in talking of such extraordinary moments of mystical ecstasy) rule out development and growth. The interior life, whether seen as the life of faith or as a moment of mystical vision, cannot be meaningfully conceived as a retirement from moral and spiritual evolution.

What, then, can fulfilment be? How might we think of what Christians have traditionally called "Last Things"? In particular, how are we to understand heaven? Surely heaven must be an ongoing fulfilment, a fulfilment that has already begun but that can never end, never be said to have reached the point where no more development can take place. For that would be indeed extinction, the extinction, that is, of the moral consciousness and the spiritual or interior life. Such extinction, I have already suggested, is hell. To stop growing in love is to stop loving. The classic distinctions made are between life *in via* (the present pilgrimage) and the life *in patria* (heaven, our true homeland), between the Church Militant here on earth and the Church Triumphant there in heaven. But the model is inapplicable. It presupposes an abnormal battle situation that at death gives place to a normal life of ease and peace. The traditional Catholic prayer is that those who have gone beyond this life may rest in peace: *requiescant in pace*. Isaiah, however, suggests a different hope: "Young men," he says, "may grow tired and weary, youths may stumble, but those who hope in Yahweh renew their strength, they put out wings like eagles. They run and do not grow weary, walk and never tire."[3] Might not we find here a more intelligible model for a concept of heaven, as that state of fulfilment that has already begun and can never end because with each fulfilment I am inevitably thrust forward to an expanded life?

In such a vision there is no question, of course, of absorption into God or of any other kind of deification. In keeping with the whole biblical tradition, it maintains the eternal gulf between God and his creatures. Nor could there ever be any danger of "catching up" with God: even to suggest that is to see God as part of the stream of which he is the source, part of the process of which he is the fount, part of the creaturely order of which he is the Creator, the Eternal One. The medieval schoolmen caught a glimpse of all this in their distinction between *eternitas* and *aeviternitas*, between eternity and endless time. Expressions such as $\epsilon i s$ $\tau o v s$ $a i \omega v a s$ and $\tau \omega v$ $a i \omega v \omega v$, which occur frequently in the New Testament, and have been variously rendered by phrases such as "for ever" and "world without end," do not necessarily refer to the eternal order of God, which can never be that of a creature. So when we talk of "the life everlasting" we talk of nothing that in any way injures the gulf that lies between creature and Creator. We are talking, rather, of a life that goes on and on endlessly. An ambiguity arises because of a notion that is separate and distinct from that of such ongoing life: the notion that eternity impinges on time. This is, of course, a central concept in Christian faith. Christ is the point at which God enters into the spatio-temporal order. In so doing he redeems us; but the redemption does not consist in lifting us out of the temporal order and putting us in the eternal one. That would be divinization, which I take to be radically incompatible with all biblical teaching. It follows, therefore, that whatever be the future that lies in store for me, it must be a temporal future, as the past can only be a temporal past. What other kind of past or future could there be? To talk of the future life as everlasting is to say it is not eternal but (to use medieval language) "aeviternal" or of infinite time.

The fulfilment to which I may look forward, whatever it be, must take place, therefore, in time. In what does it consist? How can we know, when most of us are doubtful about even the next step and must therefore in our prayers echo that of Newman: "one step enough for me." In thinking of the future life, Whittier's well-known lines come over and over again to mind: "I only know I cannot drift beyond his love and care." I walk in faith, seeing (in Paul's words) "through a glass, darkly; but then face to face: now I know in part; but then shall I know even as also I am known."[4] The traditional formulation of Christian faith is that when, being at last fully grown, having attained the fullness of my being, I become capable of the Beatific Vision, I shall enjoy that vision for ever. Surely "to see" God *is* to see him for ever. Beyond that, however, I can specify no more. I cannot and must not presume to chart the celestial geography. I know only in faith that I shall be "with Christ, which is far better."[5]

Yet while acknowledging the necessity for such reticence and recognizing the peculiar moral and spiritual value of walking in faith, one step at a time, and in gratitude to the One who illumines that step, I cannot ignore the logical consequences of the belief that the fulfilment to which I look forward must be in time.[6] There may indeed be a fulfilment at the consummation of the present aeon, in which I might hope to attain a new kind of embodiment, a new kind of *soma* that would be the instrument of that fulfilment. Already we see an analogy for this in the history of biological evolution, which does not proceed without a discontinuous as well as a continuous element. Man, for instance, did not emerge from his simian ancestors by way of a steady process like the unfolding of a daisy's petals toward the light of day. Somehow or other, man made an evolutionary leap, transforming himself in such a way that he has, for instance, the symbol-making capacity that enables him to think and to talk, to laugh and to weep, which no other animal can do at all, though even the lowest grade of humans can.[7] So, then, I might hope to achieve a fulfilment in which, being "raised up through Christ" at the end of the present age, I entered into a new state of being as far beyond my present imagining as is any paradise or heaven. In such a state I could see God and enjoy his presence as never before, so fulfilling the promises of Christ to those whom he has redeemed by his blood. Such a state would be final *in respect of the present age*; but if, as Origen held, this is but one aeon among many, why should not I go on being "changed from glory into glory" as aeon succeeds aeon?

Such a view entails no cyclic philosophy of history. On the contrary, what I have in mind excludes such a theory. There are, of course, cyclic *tendencies* in human history, just as there are cyclic tendencies in every individual's history. That I tend to repeat mistakes I have made in the past is, however, merely a psychological observation, like the commonplace that we are all creatures of habit. What makes my personal development possible is the fact that at least occasionally I succeed in breaking my habits and doing something novel that transforms me. Of course empires rise and fall. Little empires rose and fell long before the Roman Empire emerged. A Christian might well say, however, that the last empire will not fall, being transformed into something fundamentally superior to any earthly empire, as man is superior to any of his ancestors. Augustine thought he saw that transformation taking place in the yielding of the earthly city to the City of God, the Church, the New Jerusalem, which would eventually become the Kingdom of God.

Man, no doubt, has changed little in his natural tendencies and habits for thousands of years. Yet in the remote past something occurred in the evolutionary process to bring man into being. We have not the slightest reason to suppose that this humanity, so far the crowning point of the evolutionary process on this planet, ever evolved before or ever will evolve again. We know, however, that it has an ancestry. In the light of this knowledge, surely we may usefully interpret the Christian hope: man will have a progeny superior to himself. A transformation will take place that will be the end of man *as he now is* and the consummation of *his* world. Man will have to achieve this transformation himself, for there is no other way in which any progress, not least any moral progress, can be made. Yet of course the Christian good news is that while without the redeeming work of Christ we could not hope to accomplish that self-transformation of humanity, with Christ we can and we shall. Through Christ we have the means to stop the process of entropy and, by appropriating the fruits of his redeeming work, attain whatever there is to be attained when we "rise again with Christ."

Long before Teilhard was writing (indeed about the time he was born), Henry Drummond (1851-97) wrote: "Hitherto Evolution had no future. It was a pillar with marvellous carving, growing richer and finer towards the top, but without a capital; a pyramid, the vast base buried in the inorganic, towering higher and higher, tier upon tier, life above life, mind above mind, ever more perfect in its workmanship, more noble in its symmetry, and yet withal so much the more mysterious in its aspiration. The most curious eyes, following it upwards, saw nothing. . . .But the work begun by Nature is finished by the Supernatural—as we are wont to call the higher natural. And as the veil is lifted by Christianity it strikes men dumb with wonder. For the goal of Evolution is Jesus Christ.''[8] Drummond saw human history as the continuation of evolution on another level, which, having an antecedent, must also have a consequent. As a convinced Christian, he interpreted the consequent in terms of the Christian concept of the coming Kingdom of God. As in the lower stages of evolution, so in this higher one: "many are called, but few are chosen."[9]

I do not see how a modern Christian eschatology can avoid the kind of considerations Drummond had in mind. Nor do I see how anyone whose faith precludes (as does all Christian faith) all dabbling in fantastic gnosiologies can exclude from his mind the possibility, if not the likelihood, that the evolutionary process that brought mankind into being is one that is to go on interminably. But what, then, becomes of the nature of Christ's work? Surely the basic answer to such a question must be that since it has to do with the redemption of man, it will be finished, *so far as man is concerned*, with the consummation of the world that is man's milieu. What we are to be is in the nature of the case beyond our present ken except that to the eyes of faith it will be "in Christ" and therefore, as Paul says, "far better."[10] Yet surely for creatures (that is, all entities other than God, the ground and source of all being) our condition could not be "far better" if it excluded the possibility of further development. When Catholics say, as they sometimes do, that there is "no religion in heaven," they mean, of course, that there is no religion as we know it, for such religion has been transcended. That is to say, for example, that there are no sacraments such as the Church administers here on earth, for they, with all the rest of the means of salvation, would be inappropriate. Yet that is not to say there may not be other means, adapted to another and a better Household of Faith, designed to help the "hundred and forty-four thousand" victorious ones to the next stage in their evolution. Who can tell what such means might be, since we cannot tell what this "heaven" is to be, much less the "heavens" that lie beyond it? Well may mankind pray: "one aeon enough for us."

So much for the destiny of many. But what of *my* destiny? If salvation is to have any meaning for me it must speak to me not only of man but of me. All doctrines of immortality in all the great religions of the world have been concerned with personal salvation, however that salvation may have been conceived. The question to which they address themselves is the one the jailkeeper addressed to Paul and Silas: "Sirs, what must I do to be saved?"[1] If Western thought has achieved anything at all, it has developed an awareness of the peculiar value of creativity and novelty, of individuality and personhood. The awareness presents us, however, with a paradox: in humanity, the highest level of the evolutionary process that we know, both individuation and aggregation seem to be involved. The more I try to attain individuality apart from society, the more hopeless my quest becomes. The more I seek social values apart from the needs and concerns of the individual, the more impossible my undertaking is quickly seen to be. Individuality and personality depend, for their development, on the society in which the individual must struggle to free himself.

This polarity has illuminating counterparts in the history of religious development. For example, in the history of the thought and life of the Middle Ages in the Latin West, we find two tendencies strongly at work: on the one hand an introspective, contemplative attitude, which was a heritage of the Neoplatonic tradition transmitted by Augustine; on the other, a startlingly earthy, land-conscious, practical, common-sense attitude that had its roots in close contact with the soil and its life in the constant battle with the recalcitrant forces of nature. Our medieval ancestors were too close to nature to worship it. They also felt themselves too close to the ancient world to be content with it. "We are like dwarfs standing on the shoulders of giants," they said, alluding to the ancient world whose institutions they had inherited but had transformed.[12] The medieval mind was deeply conscious, in its own very special way, of the polarity apart from which nothing creative can emerge because no freedom can be exercised. One cannot liberate oneself without a prison to be liberated from. The Spanish mystics likewise saw the truth of all this in their way: in telling the mystical aspirant to renounce imagery, they recognized that he must first have imagery to renounce.

So, then, whatever is uniquely *me* has been developed out of struggle with the society in which I discover myself. What emerges is the peculiar dimension of energy the ancients groped to designate when they talked of the soul of man. It is that kind of energy that brings us in the long run into deeper communion with God who, far from being "the Absolute" of so much traditional idealist thought, is individual *par excellence*: in Kierkegaard's tellingly odd idiom, he is "pure subjectivity." That individuality, that personality that is leaping out of what is superficially called "me" is the energy in me that cannot die and must find embodiment, perhaps many thousands of times before "the end of the age." The energy is immortalized by the peculiar direction it has taken. It is not energy that is spent in the exercise of power, for that kind of energy, though it may play a part in the moral development of the individual, is burnt up like any other form of energy. It is, on the contrary, the energy that is created by the abdication of power. Hence the Gospel paradox: "He that findeth his life shall lose it; and he that loseth his life for my sake shall find it."[13] Love, which entails sacrifice, the abdication of self-centered power, immortalizes energy by putting it into the trusteeship of God. So self-renunciation, far from inhibiting me, enables me, rather, "to turn again and live."[14]

The total absence of such energy (the energy that has begun, at least, to turn into that sacrificial love that is indestructible), would lead to hell, which I interpret as final extinction. If, however, one dies with even as much as a slight sign of the budding of the capacity for the love that puts us into communion with the self-emptying One we call God, then one will surely seek and find re-embodiment through which to love him more. I see no reason why a Christian should not at least entertain the suggestion that the re-embodiment should occur over and over again, giving the individual opportunity to grow in the love of God. That re-embodiment I would call reincarnation. I am inclined to think the concept of reincarnation is, indeed, the key to a fuller Christian understanding of human destiny. Of course primitive forms of reincarnationism must be discarded. In the history of religious ideas, outmoded formulations are continually giving place to more adequate ones. The temptation of throwing the baby out with the bath water is familiar, however, to all historians of ideas, religious or otherwise. Religious revolutionaries often succumb to it; but so even more do those ideophobiacs who hug ancient formulations till they petrify, yet will not tolerate the new formulations that could restore and develop religious life. Could not it be that reincarnationism, which has taken such well-known primitive forms, might have been a particularly unfortunate casualty? I would suggest that Christians and others to whom reincarnationism seems alien might do well to re-examine it in case a new formulation of it should be found to provide a vast flood of light on the eschatological muddle that has haunted the history of Christian thought.

I see myself drawn forth in the course of my present life from the amorality of self-centeredness to a much deeper sense of the love of God, with the peculiar kind of moral vivacity that such a development always brings. I remember vividly the prison of that self-centeredness and know so well how far the grace of God has taken me in my struggle for freedom. Yet for all the vast progress I see, I know I have farther to go than I can hope to go in this life. It is not merely a matter of time. If gerontology could prolong my active and useful life by a thousand years, my predicament would remain. For the youthful idealism needed for the most active development of the love of God wanes. A great saint might become even saintlier than ever in his nineties; but even he would not do it as fast as he had done it in his prime. I need, therefore, another embodiment, and it seems to me that the more progress I make through such re-embodiments the more need for them shall I see, as the more progress I make in courage or learning the more easily I perceive how cowardly or ignorant I am.

Each reincarnation is, of course, a resurrection. The resurrection that is promised to those who are made partakers of the resurrection of Christ is not only preserved as the Christian hope; it can now be seen as a continuing process in which every rebirth gives me new capacity for walking closer and closer with God. At the end of every aeon there might well be a special evolutionary "leap", a unique step in the infinite pilgrimage toward God. I cannot know; but what I know of my past, and even of the moral and spiritual development in my own life on earth suggests to me that such "leaps" might occur at the end of every age of cosmic history.

Then what does Christ do for me? The answer for the Christian is surely simple. He does what Christian evangelists have always said he does: he liberates me from the burden of my sins, the guilt of which would block my progress. So I am enabled, being restored to health, to struggle on toward the fuller appropriation of the love of God. In short, Christ may be seen, as Christians have always seen him, as providing me with the conditions for freeing myself. If that seems little, then it must seem little to be extinguished for ever. If Christ's work seems of no account, then existence itself must seem unimportant. If, when I am a slave in chains, my fetters are broken and the door of my prison opened, I do not grumble because I am not then taken to a good tailor and to a fashionable restaurant for dinner. Surely I am content to celebrate the "amazing grace" that broke my chains and has made me able to use the abundant energy that has become available to me.

We may conclude that there is nothing in biblical thought or Christian tradition that necessarily excludes all forms of reincarnationism. We have seen many historical reasons why it has been suppressed both officially and at the popular level, in the history of the Christian Church. We have seen no reason why it must be in conflict with the historic teachings that have come to us through the Bible and the Church. We have seen, above all, that some form of reincarnationism could much enhance the spirituality of the West, not least at the present time when it stands so much in need of fresh avenues of development and new means of illumination.

REFERENCES AND NOTES

[1] It is specifically suggested by Clement of Alexandria as early as the second century. See *Stromata, 7.6.*

[2] Genesis 1.1.

[3] Isaiah 40.31 (JB).

[4] I Corinthians 13.12 (KJV).

[5] Philippians 1.23 (KJV).

[6] Psalm 119.105.

[7] For a discussion of some questions relating to the evolution of man, *see* my *Philosophical Issues in Religious Thought* (Boston: Houghton Mifflin Company, 1973), pp. 189 ff.

[8] Henry Drummond, *Natural Law in the Spiritual World* (New York: Pott, 1904), p. 303. The original edition appeared in 1883. Drummond, who was also well-known as a geologist and explorer in America and Africa, was a Scottish churchman and evangelist. He was among the many distinguished people of his day who were interested in the work of the Society for Psychical Research.

[9] Matthew 22.14.

[10] Philippians 1.23.

[11] Acts 16.30.

[12] The saying is attributed to several medieval writers, including Peter of Blois.

[13] Matthew: 10.39.

[14] For an expression of this paradox in psychological terms, *see* a striking chapter by the distinguished Swiss physician and psychotherapist, Paul Tournier, *The Meaning of Persons* (New York: Harper and Row, 1957), p. 217.

BIBLIOGRAPHY

Abhedananda, Swami. *Reincarnation*. Calcutta: Ramakrishna Vedanta Math, 1968. First Published 1899.

Alger, William R. *Destiny of the Soul: A Critical History of the Doctrine of a Future Life,* 2 vols. New York: Greenwood, 1968.
  The original edition, published in 1860, was for long regarded as the standard work on its subject. Its author, a Unitarian minister, included a bibliography of nearly 5,000 works. He accounted the case for reincarnation very strong.

Anderson, A. R., ed. *Minds and Machines*. Englewood Cliffs, N.J.: Prentice-Hall, Inc., 1964.
  Critical studies of the mind-body problem.

Aurobindo, Sri. *The Problem of Rebirth*. Pondicherri, India: Sri Aurobindo Ashram, 1952.
  A provocative collection of essays on karma and reincarnation by a very original Indian thinker.

Baillie, John. *And the Life Everlasting*. New York: Oxford University Press, 1966.
  First published in 1934. A well-known treatment of immortality by a Scottish Presbyterian divine.

Berdyaev, Nicolas. *The Destiny of Man*. New York: Charles Scribner's Sons, 1937.
  Part III of this work by one of the most interesting religious thinkers of the twentieth century, a Russian who, after a period of skepticism, with Marxist leanings, returned to the Orthodox Church, contains his thought on Death and Immortality. He is much disposed to reincarnationism: *see* his remarks on karma, p. 349.

Bergson, Henri. *Mind-Energy*. New York: Henry Holt and Co., 1960.
  Tr. H. W. Carr of *L'Energie spirituelle,* first published 1919, by this important French philosopher.

Bernstein, Morey. *The Search for Bridey Murphy*. Garden City, New York: Doubleday and Co., Inc., 1956.

Besant, Annie. *The Ancient Wisdom*. Adyar, Madras: Theosophical Publishing House, 1939.
   By one of the early leaders of the theosophical movement in the nineteenth century.

Blanshard, Brand. *The Nature of Thought,* Vol. I. London: George Allen and Unwin, Ltd., 1939.
   A critical study of the mind-body problem by one of the most eminent of contemporary American thinkers.

Blavatsky, H. P. *Isis Unveiled*. Pasadena, California: Theosophical University Press, 1963.
_____. *The Secret Doctrine*. Pasadena, California: Theosophical University Press, 1963.
   Reprints of the two major works of the founder of the nineteenth century theosophical movement.

Blythe, Henry. *The Three Lives of Naomi Henry*. New York: Citadel Press, 1957.
   First published in England in 1956. Reports claims relating to experiments in hypnotic regression to previous lives.

Bonhomme, Denise. *The Esoteric Substance of Voltairian Thought*. New York: Philosophical Library, 1974.
   A daring, not to say fantastic, attempt to "de-code" Voltaire so as to discern a theosophical outlook in his thought.

Brain, W. Russell. *Mind, Perception, and Science*. Oxford: B. H. Blackwell, Ltd., 1951.
   Critical study of the mind-body problem.

Brazzini, Pasquale. *Dopo la morte si rinasce?* Milan: Fratelli Bocca Editori, 1952.
   Contains a report of the case of Giuseppe Costa from the latter's autobiography.

Broad, C. D. *The Mind and Its Place in Nature*. London: Routledge and Kegan Paul, Ltd., 1925.
   A classic work by an important Cambridge philosopher.

Brunner, Constantin. *Science, Spirit, Superstition*. London: George Allen and Unwin, Ltd., 1968.
   Chapter IV contains some interesting comments on problems relating to metempsychosis and the development of thought in the foetus.

Caianiello, E. R., ed. *Lectures on the Field Theory and the Many-Body Problem*. New York: Academic Press, 1961.

Carrington, Whateley. *Telepathy*. London: Methuen and Co., Ltd., 1945.
   See especially cc.6-8 on how we are constantly influencing each other, at the unconscious level. The work is valuable as a survey of the experimental work on telepathy.

Céline, Louis-Ferdinand. *Death on the Installment Plan*. New York: New Directions, 1971.
   Tr. R. Manhein. First published 1966. Paperback edition.

Cerminara, Gina. *Many Mansions*. New York: William Sloane Associates, Inc., 1950.
  Based on the "life readings" of Edgar Cayce.
_____. *The World Within*. New York: W. Sloane Associates, Inc., 1957.
_____. *Many Lives, Many Loves*. New York: W. Sloane Associates, Inc., 1963.

Chari, C. T. K. "Paramnesia and Reincarnation". In *Proceedings of the Society for Psychical Research*, Vol. 53, December, 1962.
_____. "Paranormal Cognition, Survival and Reincarnation". In *Journal of the American Society for Psychical Research*, Vol. 56, No. 4, October, 1962.

Cullmann, Oscar. *Immortality of the Soul or Resurrection from the Dead?* New York: Macmillan Co., 1958.
  A particularly useful discussion.

Dalai Lama. *My Land and My People*. New York: McGraw-Hill Book Company, 1962.
  Includes an account of the finding and testing of the fourteenth Dalai Lama.

de Rochas, A. *Les Vies successives*. Paris: Librairie Générale des Sciences Occultes, 1924.
  A pioneer work on hypnotic regression experiments purporting to disclose previous lives.

de Silva, Lynn A. *The Problem of the Self in Buddhism and Christianity*. Colombo, Sri Lanka: Study Center for Religion and Society, 1975. A particularly interesting study of the question, not least Chapter XII: "Progressive Sanctification After Death".

Delanne, Gabriel. *Documents pour servir à l'étude de la Réincarnation*. Paris: Editions de la B. P. S., 1924.
  Contains information about claims to reincarnation.

Des Georges, A. *La Réincarnation des âmes selon les traditions orientales et occidentales*. Paris: Editions Albin Michel, 1966.
  A review of the belief in reincarnation among various peoples.

Deschamps, H. *Les Religions de l'Afrique noire*. Paris: Presses Universitaires de France, 1970.

Ducasse, C. J. "How the case of *The Search for Bridey Murphy* stands today". In *Journal of the American Society for Psychical Research*, Vol. 54, 1960.
_____. *Nature, Mind, and Death*. La Salle, Illinois: Open Court Publishing Co., 1951.
  Critical study of the mind-body problem by a well-known American philosopher.
_____. *A Critical Examination of the Belief in a Life After Death*. Springfield, Illinois: Charles C. Thomas, 1961.
  Contains a critical review of the evidence for reincarnation, with a chapter on the Bridey Murphy case.

Egerton, C. Baptist. *Nibbāna or the Kingdom,* 2nd. ed. Colombo: Gunasena, 1964.

Evans-Wentz, W. Y. *Tibetan Yoga and Secret Doctrines.* London: Oxford University Press, 1935.
    Extensive references to reincarnation in this remarkable Oxford scholar's great work.
_____. *The Tibetan Book of the Dead.* London: Oxford University Press, 1927.

Feyerabend, H., and Maxwell, G., ed. *Mind, Matter, and Method.* Minneapolis: University of Minnesota Press, 1966.
    A useful study of the mind-body problem.

Flew, A., ed., *Body, Mind, and Death.* New York: Crowell-Collier and MacMillan, Inc., 1962.

Gould, B. *The Jewel in the Lotus.* London: Chatto and Windus, 1957.
    Contains an account of the finding and testing of the fourteenth Dalai Lama.

Govinda, Lama Anagarika. *The Way of the White Clouds.* London: Hutchinson and Co., 1966.
    Autobiography of a German-born Tibetan Buddhist. Contains a report of claims to memory of a previous life.

Haich, Elisabeth. *Initiation.* London: George Allen and Unwin, Ltd., 1965.
    Contains, in the form of a novel, an account of claims to memory of a previous life.

Hall, H. Fielding. *The Soul of a People.* London: Macmillan and Co., Ltd., 1922.
    First published 1898. Contains six case histories of Burmese children who claimed memory of previous lives.

Harrer, H. *Seven Years in Tibet.* New York: E. P. Dutton and Co., 1954.
    Tr. R. Graves. Contains an account of the finding and testing of the fourteenth Dalai Lama.

Harvey-Day, H. "Reincarnation: Have We Proof?" In *Prediction,* V, August. 1940, pp. 252-258.

Head, Joseph, and Cranston, S. L. *Reincarnation and World Thought.* New York: Julian Press, 1967.

_____, *Reincarnation: an East-West Anthology.* Wheaton: The Theosophical Publishing House, 1968.

Hearn, Lafcadio. *Gleanings in Buddha Fields.* London: Jonathan Cape, 1927.
    First published 1897. Contains a chapter documenting the claim of a Japanese boy in the early nineteenth century to memory of a previous life.

Hedde, R. "Métempsycose". In *Dictionnaire de Théologie Catholique,*

Vol. X(2).
Extensive historical review and considerable discussion.

Hick, John. *Death and Eternal Life.* London: Collins, 1976.

Hiriyanna, M. *The Essentials of Indian Philosophy.* London: George Allen and Unwin, 1949.
Probably still the best brief introduction in English to Indian thought.

Howe, Jr., Quincy. *Reincarnation for the Christian.* Philadelphia: Westminster Press, 1974.
A helpful introduction to the question, though inadequately sensitive to the complexities of Christian theology, tradition and experience.

Hoyle, Fred. *Man and Materialism.* London: George Allen and Unwin, 1957.

Hume, R. E. *The Thirteen Principal Upanishads.* London: Oxford University Press, 1921.
A standard edition of the most important Upanishads, in English translation.

Humphreys, Christmas. *Karma and Rebirth.* London: John Murray, 1943.

Jayatilake, K. N. "Evidences of Rebirth". In *Ceylon Today,* Vol. 13, May, 1964, p. 19.

Jung, C. G. *Psychology and Religion: West and East* (Collected Works). Edited by H. Read. London: Routledge and Kegan Paul, 1958.
Tr. R. F. C. Hull. Contains some discussion of karma and reincarnation from a Jungian standpoint.

_____. *Symbols of Transformation*, 2 vols. New York: Harper Torchbooks, 1956.
Chapter V contains a psychoanalytical discussion of the role of symbols of rebirth.

Kant, Immanuel. *Critique of Practical Reason.*
See Book II, Chapters 2-5, for discussion of immortality.

Kapleau, Philip. *The Wheel of Death.* New York: Harper, 1971. Writings from Zen and other sources. Bibliography.

Kardec, Allan. *Le Livre des médiums.* Paris: Didier et Cie., 1862.
A pioneering work on spiritism; refers to reincarnation. Of historical interest.

Kelsey, Deny and Grant. *Many Lifetimes.* Garden City, New York: Doubleday and Co., 1967.

Keyfitz, N. "How many people have lived on earth?" In *Demography,* Vol. 3, 1966, p. 581.
Refers to a frequently asked question about reincarnation.

Lewis, H. D. "Mind and Body". In *Clarity Is Not Enough.* London: George Allen and Unwin, 1963.
A good study of the mind-body problem by a British philosopher.

_____. *The Self and Immortality*. New York: Seabury Press, 1973.
Argues that a neo-Cartesian interactionist theory of mind/body
relationship does better justice to human experience than do theories of
mind/brain identity, such as that of the late Gilbert Ryle. Chapter VI on
Reincarnation is especially relevant to the present study.

Long, Herbert Strainge. *A Study of the Doctrine of Metempsychosis in
Greece: From Pythagoras to Plato*. New Jersey: Princeton University
Press, 1948.

Lutoslawski, Wincenty. *Pre-existence and Reincarnation*. London:
Allen and Unwin, 1928.

MacKinnon, D. M. "Death". In *New Essays in Philosophical Theology*.
Edited by A. MacIntyre, and A. G. N. Flew, London: S. C. M. Press,
1955.
A well-known article by a Cambridge philosopher.

Marcel, Gabriel. *Presence and Immortality*. Pittsburgh: Duquesne Uni-
versity Press, 1967.
Tr. M. A. Machado. Reflections on immortality by a leading French
Catholic existentialist.

Martin, Eva. *Reincarnation: The Ring of Return*. New Hyde Park, New
York: University Books, 1963.
First published in England 1927.

Mascaró, Juan. *The Bhagavad Gita*. London: Penguin Books, 1962.
An English translation with an admirable introduction by the translator.

Moody, Jr., Raymond A. *Life After Life*. New York: Bantam Books,
1975.
Discusses cases of persons who have "died" and "returned" to life,
with their accounts of the experience of dying, whose testimony is
remarkably similar and includes allusion to moving down a dark tunnel
and to encounter with a "Being of Light". There is a striking affinity
with the findings of Elisabeth Kubler-Ross, M.D., who contributes a
foreword. They had not met till after the book was written. It does not
purport to offer "proof" of an after-life.

Moore, George Foot. *Metempsychosis*. Cambridge, Mass.: Harvard University Press, 1914.
Discusses metempsychosis in various cultures, especially in Greece.

Morgan, Kenneth, ed. *The Religion of the Hindus*. New York: Ronald
Press, 1953.
An account of the beliefs and practices of the Hindus by devotees.

Myers, F. W. H. *Human Personality and Its Survival of Bodily Death*.
New Hyde Park, New York: University Books, Inc., 1961.
A classic in psychical research, first published 1903. Contains (p. 293
ff.) a critique of reincarnationism from the standpoint of an eminent
pioneer in psychical research.

Nair, K. Bhaskharan. "Reincarnation". In *Adhyatma Saroj,* I, July, 1965, pp. 37-39.

Neidhart, Georg. *Werden Wir Wieder Geboren?* Munich: Gemeinschaft für Religiöse und Geistige Eerneurung, 1956.
    Contains report of a claim to memory of a life in twelfth century Bavaria.

Origen. *Contra Celsum.* Translated by H. Chadwick. Cambridge: Cambridge University Press, 1953.
_____. *On First Principles.* Translated by G. W. Butterworth. New York: Harper and Row, 1966.

Parrinder, E. G. "Varieties of Belief in Reincarnation". In *Hibbert Journal,* Vol. 55, 1956, pp. 260-267.

Pelikan, Jaroslav. *The Shape of Death.* Nashville, Tennessee: Abingdon Press, 1961.
    A concise work on death and immortality in the Christian Fathers by a well-known Yale scholar. Provocative suggestion for the classification of patristic thought on immortality.

Penelhum, Terence. *Religion and Rationality.* New York: Random House, 1971.
    See Chapters XXIV ("Survival") and XXV ("The Possibility of Life after Death"). Sympathetic and critical treatment by a professional philosopher.

_____, *Survival and Disembodied Existence.* London: Routledge and Kegan, 1970.

Phillips, D. Z. *Death and Immortality.* London: Macmillan and Co., Ltd., 1970.
    An admirably succinct review of current philosophical discussion.

Pinart, A. "Esquimaux et Koloches: Idées religieuses et traditions des Kaniagmioutes". In *Revue d'Anthropologie,* Vol. 4, 1873, pp. 647-680.

Prabhupādha, (Bhaktivedanta Swami). *Bhagavad-gītā As It Is.* New York: Collier Books, 1972.
    An edition with Sanskrit text, English translation, and "purports" by the spiritual leader of the Krishna-consciousness movement. Reincarnation is a dominant theme.

Praed, Campbell. *The Soul of Nyria.* London: Rider and Co., 1931.
    Report of claim to memory of a previous life in ancient Rome.

Radhakrishnan, Sarvepalli. *Eastern Religions and Western Thought.* New York: Oxford University Press, 1959.
    Interesting study by a very prominent Hindu.

Reeves, J. W., ed. *Body and Mind in Western Thought.* Baltimore: Penguin Books, Inc., 1958.
    Very useful study of the mind-body problem in the history of Western philosophy.

Reyna, Ruth. *Reincarnation and Science*. New Delhi: Sterling Publishers PVT, Ltd., 1973.
A critical study of alleged empirical evidence for reincarnation.
_____. "Reincarnation: Is It a Hoax or a Reality?" In *Illustrated Weekly of India*, January 8, 1967, pp. 51-53.

Rhine, J. B. *New Frontiers of the Mind*. New York: Farrar and Rinehart, Inc., 1937.
An important work on telepathy.

Rhine, Louisa E. "Review of Ian Stevenson, *Twenty Cases Suggestive of Reincarnation*". In *Journal of Parapsychology*, Vol. 30, No. 4, December, 1966, pp. 263-272.
See also under Stevenson, Ian.

Roberts, Jane. *The Seth Material*. Englewood Cliffs, N.J.: Prentice-Hall, 1970.

Routh, H. V. "This World's Idea of the Next" (Tredegar Memorial Lecture). In *Essays by Divers Hands*, Vol. XXV (new series). London: Oxford University Press, 1950.

Russell, Bertrand. *Religion and Science*. New York: Oxford University Press, 1961. (Galaxy Books; first published 1935.)
Chapter V ("Soul and Body") provides an excellent statement, in untechnical language, of the philosophical and scientific difficulties about personal immortality, yet without dogmatic opposition to it. Every beginner should read this chapter.

Ryall, E., *Born Twice: Recall of a Seventeenth Century Life*. New York: Harper and Row, 1975.

Ryle, Gilbert. *The Concept of Mind*. London: Hutchinson and Co., Ltd., 1949.
A very influential critique of traditional notions about the soul, by an Oxford philosopher.

Sahay, K. K. N. *Reincarnation: Verified Cases of Rebirth After Death*. Bareilly, India: Privately printed, 1927.
Contains seven reports of Indian cases.

Schilleebeeckx, E., and Willems, B., ed. *The Problem of Eschatology* (*Concilium*, Vol. 41). New York: Paulist Press, 1969.

Schrödinger, Erwin, *Mind and Matter*. Cambridge: Cambridge University Press, 1958.

Shaffer, Jerome. "Recent Work on the Mind-Body Problem". In *American Philosophical Quarterly*, II, 1965, pp. 81-104.

Shirley, Ralph. *The Problem of Rebirth*. London: Occult Book Society.

Siwek, Paul. *The Enigma of the Hereafter*. New York: Philosophical Library, 1952.
Hostile, but contains some useful information.

Smart, Ninian. *The Religious Experience of Mankind*. New York:

Charles Scribner's Sons, 1969.
   A text on the history of religions, containing ((pp. 73 ff.) some discussion of reincarnation in Jain teaching, and also (pp. 303 ff.) a brief account of the reincarnationist notions of the kabbalist Isaac Luria (1514-1572).
   The author is a professor at the University of Lancaster, England.

Soal, S. G. *The Experimental Situation in Psychical Research.* London: The Society for Psychical Research, 1947. *See also* his papers in the Society's *Proceedings* (XLVI, 152-198 and XLVII, 21-150), in which he reports positive results for pre-cognitive telepathy with odds against chance of billions to one.

Spencer, Frederick A. M. *The Future Life: A New Interpretation of the Christian Doctrine.* London: Hamish Hamilton, 1935.
   Contains discussions which, though outmoded, are exceptionally interesting as showing the development of the notion of "evolutionary immortality" in modern times. *See* especially Ch. X ("The Doctrine of Metempsychosis") and Ch. XI ("Evolutionary Immortality"). The latter contains references to a letter by Cardinal Mercier acknowledging that belief in pre-existence and reincarnation had not been formally condemned by the Church as heretical, addressed to a Polish Catholic, Professor Wincenty Lutoslawski, who taught a form of reincarnationism that he preferred to call palingenesis.

Stearn, Jess. *The Search for the Girl with the Blue Eyes.* Garden City, New York: Doubleday, 1968.

Steiger, B., and Williams, L. G., *Other Lives.* New York: Award Books, 1969. Reports on people who, under hypnosis, claim reincarnation.

Steiner, Rudolf. *The Manifestation of Karma.* London: Rudolf Steiner Publishing Company, 1947.
   The author, at one time a German leader of the theosophical movement, became the founder of a movement called anthroposophy.

Stendahl, Krister, ed., *Immortality and Resurrection.* New York: The Macmillan Company, 1965.
   Four important Ingersoll lectures at Harvard.

Stevenson, Ian, M. D. "Twenty Cases Suggestive of Reincarnation". In *Proceedings of the American Society for Psychical Research,* Vol. 26, 1966, pp. 1-362.
   An important contribution by an outstanding researcher.
_____. "The Evidence for Survival from Claimed Memories of Former Incarnations". In *Journal of the American Society for Psychical Research,* Vol. 54, 1960, pp. 51-71, 95-117.

_____. "Characteristics of Cases of the Reincarnation Type in Turkey and Their Comparison with Cases in Two Other Cultures". In *International Journal of Comparative Sociology,* Vol. 11, March, 1970.

_____."Cultural Patterns in Cases Suggestive of Reincarnation Among the Tlingit Indians of Southeastern Alaska". In *Journal of the American Society for Psychical Research,* Vol. 60, July, 1966.

_____. "A Case of the Reincarnation Type in Ceylon: The Case of Disna Samarasinghe". In *Journal of Asian and African Studies,* Vol. 5, October, 1970.

_____. "Some Questions Related to Cases of the Reincarnation Type". In *Journal of the American Society for Psychical Research,* Vol. 68, October, 1974, pp. 395-413.

_____. "Reply to Dr. L. E. Rhine on her Review". In *Journal of Parapsychology,* Vol. 31, June, 1967, pp. 149-154.
    See also under Rhine, Louisa E.

Story, Francis. *The Case for Rebirth.* Kandy, Ceylon: The Buddhist Publication Society, 1959.
    Revised edition 1964.

Story, Francis, and Stevenson, Ian. "A Case of the Reincarnation Type in Ceylon". In *Journal of the American Society for Psychical Research,* Vol. 61, April, 1967.

Strawson, P. F. *Individuals.* London: Methuen and Co., Ltd., 1959.
    Important study of the mind-body problem by an Oxford philosopher.

Sugrue, Thomas. *There is a River.* New York: Henry Holt and Co., 1942.
    The story of Edgar Cayce.

Sunderlal, R. B. S. "Cas apparents de réminiscences de vies antérieures". In *Revue Métapsychique,* July/August, 1924, pp. 302-307.
    Contains four accounts of alleged Indian cases of memory of previous lives.

Tatz, Mark, and Kent, Jody. *The Tibetan Game of Liberation.* New York: Doubleday (Anchor Books), 1977.
    Presents the traditional game with Buddhist map of the universe in 104 squares.

Teilhard de Chardin, Pierre. *The Phenomenon of Man.* New York: Harper and Bros., 1959.
    A very influential work by an eminent Jesuit scientist. While it does not specifically treat reincarnation, it contains material of special interest to students of the subject.

Thera, Nyanatiloka. *Karma and Rebirth.* Kandy, Ceylon: The Buddhist Publication Society.

Thielicke, Helmut. *Death and Life.* Philadelphia: Fortress Press, 1970.
    By a distinguished German Lutheran theologian. Very unsympathetic to classic immortality theories, including reincarnationism.

Thrope, Louis F., and Schmuller, Allen M. *Personality,* (East-West edition) Princeton, N.J. : D. Van Nostrand Co., 1965.

Vesey, G. N. A. *Body and Mind.* London: George Allen and Unwin, Ltd., 1964.

Vycinas, Vincent. *Search for Gods*. The Hague: Martinus Nijhoff, 1972.
    Chapter VIII, "Reincarnation", written in a Heideggerian vein, pre-
sents karmic guilt as a kind of "illness of man's inner self."

Walker, D. P. *The Decline of Hell*. London: Routledge and Kegan Paul,
1964.
    A scholarly treatment of seventeenth century discussion of the after-
life, with valuable references to the defense of metempsychosis among
English and other writers of the period, including Henry More, Baron
Van Helmont and Viscountess Conway.

Walker, E. D. *Reincarnation: a Study of Forgotten Truth*. New Hyde
Park, N.Y.: University Books, 1965.
    First published 1888.

Wellemeyer, F., et al. "How Many People Have Ever Lived on Earth?"
In *Population Bulletin*, Vol. 18, 1962, pp. 1-19.
    Relevant to a frequently asked question about reincarnation.

Wilson, Ernest C. *Have You Lived Other Lives?* Englewood Cliffs, N.J.:
Prentice-Hall, Inc., 1956.
    A popular presentation of reincarnationist belief by a minister of the
Unity Church.

Wilson, R. McL., "Jewish Gnosis and Gnostic Origins" in *Hebrew
Union College Annual*, Vol. XLV. Cincinnati, 1974.
    Shows how Gnosticism and early Christianity overlapped.

Winkler, W. "Wie viele Menschen haben bisher auf der Erde gelebt?" In
Report of International Population Conference. Vienna: Union Inter-
nationale pour l'Etude Scientifique de la Population, 1959, pp. 73-76.

Wisdom, John. *Other Minds*. Oxford: B. H. Blackwell, Ltd., 1949.
    A well-known study by a distinguished British philosopher.

Wood, Frederick. *This Egyptian Miracle*. London: John M. Watkins,
1955.
    Reports an English medium's claim to memory of a previous life in
ancient Egypt.

Yogananda, Paramhansa. *Autobiography of a Yogi*. London: Rider and
Co., 1959.
    Contains some interesting material on reincarnation.

Zaehner, R. C. *Hinduism*. New York: Oxford University Press, 1962.
    An introduction to key concepts in Hinduism by an eminent scholar in
the history of religion.

Zahan, D., ed. *Réincarnation et vie mystique en Afrique noire*. Paris:
Presses Universitaires de France, 1965.

Books by Geddes MacGregor

He Who Lets Us Be
The Rhythm of God
Philosophical Issues in Religious Thought
So Help Me God. A Calendar of Quick Prayers for Half-Skeptics
A Literary History of the Bible
The Sense of Absence
God Beyond Doubt
The Hemlock and the Cross
The Coming Reformation
Introduction to Religious Philosophy
The Bible in the Making
Corpus Christi
The Thundering Scot
The Tichborne Impostor
The Vatican Revolution
From A Christian Ghetto: Letters of Ghostly Wit, Written
    A.D. 2453
Les Frontières de la morale et de la religion
Christian Doubt
Aesthetic Experience in Religion

INDEX

Practicality is the sole function of an index: it is for helping the reader to find quickly the passages he wishes to consult. Certain entries (e.g., *Karma,* Reincarnation, Hinduism, Christianity) would be so numerous as to be next to useless except in an elaborately analytical index, which this one is not. Completeness is therefore not the criterion by which its value is to be judged.